Praise for
Write Like You Mean It

"Steve's book is as honest, transparent, and realistic a book about writing as I've read in a very long time. His approach offers insights, advice, and sensible strategies to stop procrastinating and start writing."

—Neil Foote, Principal Lecturer, Mayborn School of Journalism, and Director, Mayborn Literary Nonfiction Conference

"Whether you're looking to get into writing seriously or are an experienced writer looking to brush up on a few things, Steve does a great job of laying things out in an easy format that communicates good information to the reader—which is what writing is all about."

—Ben Baby, NFL and Boxing Reporter, ESPN

"Steve Gamel has written a book, *Write Like You Mean It*, that gives advice based on his experience as a writer. It is a collection of practical advice useful to those trying to learn how to write and those who are trying to learn how to write better."

—Keith Shelton, Retired Writer, Professor, Lecturer, and Advisor, University of North Texas

"Steve Gamel has written a book that aspiring writers can treasure . . . a love letter to the written word."

—Scott Parks, Retired Managing Editor, *Denton Record-Chronicle*

"In *Write Like You Mean It*, Steve Gamel blazes a trail for aspiring writers. It is no surprise to find that Steve's writing itself is clear and understandable. The book is easy to read, and the stories are memorable. This guide provides numerous practical tips and suggestions to help you deal with the challenges of writing and getting published. Whether you are an experienced writer or a novice hoping to be, digest this book."

—Tim Stevenson, Master Sherpa Executive Coach
and Author of *Better: The Fundamentals of Leadership*

"*Write Like You Mean It* includes techniques and strategies valuable to writers of all ability and experience levels, and it's also a great resource for encouraging potential writers. Gamel shows how writing can be something to enjoy rather than fear and the ways a passion for writing can lead to great opportunities."

—Matt Wixon, Award-Winning Journalist
and Author of *Fourth Down in Texas* and *3 Seats from the Hero*

"Valuable as a refresher for even the most experienced writers. Gives a good overview of many nonfiction writing opportunities and sound info for fiction writers."

—Les Edgerton, Author of *Finding Your Voice* and *Hooked*

"In *Write Like You Mean It*, Steve Gamel masterfully conveys that great writing goes far beyond the construct of a great sentence. This old-school writer offers timeless tips, tricks, and techniques that will ensure the success of any new-school dreamer or veteran wordsmith. Gamel, an accomplished and award-winning writer, goes far beyond just educating the reader about a skill set . . . his guidance serves as sage advice for anyone who needs to overcome paralyzing fear or a mental block that is keeping them from taking chances in any facet of life. Gamel wrote it like he meant it!"

—Gayle Stinson, Ed.D., Superintendent of Schools for
Birdville Independent School District

WRITE

like you

MEAN IT

WRITE

like you

MEAN IT

Mastering Your Passion for the Written Word

Steve Gamel

BROWN BOOKS
PUBLISHING GROUP

Write Like You Mean It
Mastering Your Passion for the Written Word

Brown Books Publishing Group
Dallas, TX / New York, NY
www.BrownBooks.com
(972) 381-0009

A New Era in Publishing®

Publisher's Cataloging-In-Publication Data

Names: Gamel, Steve, author.
Title: Write like you mean it : mastering your passion for the written
    word / Steve Gamel.
Description: Dallas, TX ; New York, NY : Brown Books Publishing
    Group, [2021] | Includes bibliographical references.
Identifiers: ISBN 9781612545271
Subjects: LCSH: Authorship. | Journalism.
Classification: LCC PN145 .G36 2021 | DDC 808.02--dc23

ISBN 978-1-61254-527-1
LCCN 2021906867

Printed in the United States
10 9 8 7 6 5 4 3 2 1

For more information or to contact the author,
please go to www.EditThisLLC.com.

I dedicate this book to everyone who inspired me to chase my passion for writing. Also, here's to my wife—my biggest fan, even if she has yet to read anything I've written start to finish. If that changes with this book, then I know that I have truly made it as a writer.

Contents

Start Writing!

Writing to a Purpose

Write Like You Mean It to Be Read

Foreword

Scott Parks

Steve Gamel has written a book that aspiring writers can treasure. He invites us into a world in which each word must fit together perfectly one after the other. The writer is like the cabinetmaker who strives to build the perfect chest of drawers. The pieces of wood must fit together seamlessly. The drawers must slide in and out as if they were riding on air.

To enter Steve's world is like gaining membership to an exclusive club of master craftsmen. Words and stories are their stock in trade. They describe the nature of beauty. They delve into the roots of love and hate. They want to help others understand the seemingly incomprehensible world around them. They revel in the idea that their writing illuminates dark corners. Or they may want to describe a football game by constructing a story that has a beginning, middle, and end.

After writing his American masterpiece *The Great Gatsby*, F. Scott Fitzgerald knelt down before the written word and proclaimed his allegiance. "I've found my line," he wrote. "From now on, this comes first. This is my immediate duty—without this I am nothing."

Steve's book amounts to a love letter to the written word. He shows us the keys that unlock good writing. He knows the quest will never end. Writers go to their graves knowing their work could have been better. They see no perfection in themselves but revel in the perfection of other writers. They find inspiration in prose, poetry, song lyrics, and even advertising copy on an outdoor billboard or in a magazine.

Hank Williams, the god of country music, was a genius who could write a perfect song on a cocktail napkin in twenty minutes. Savor the lyrics of "I'm So Lonesome I Could Cry," which he wrote at age twenty-five.

> *I've never seen a night so long*
> *When time goes crawling by*
> *The moon just went behind the clouds*
> *To hide its face and cry.*

I spent forty-five years writing for newspapers and television news. And I never wrote anything as beautiful and exquisite as "I'm So Lonesome I Could Cry." Even so, I am still trying. I'm still a student. I picked out more than a few nuggets in Steve's book that will help improve my writing—for example, that we writers must set aside our shyness and show our work to fellow writers so that their comments and criticisms can help lift a work out of the weeds and help us see our work in a wider perspective. Steve reminds us of Hemingway's warning that the first draft of anything is worthless: a manuscript becomes fully baked only after many rewrites. He doesn't sugarcoat the tedium of writing.

Still, this book exists to help everyone who feels compelled to get thoughts out of their head and onto paper in a coherent form that connects with readers. I'm gratified that Steve asked me to write this foreword. I wish I could have written it better.

Introduction

"The secret of getting ahead is getting started."
—Mark Twain

On the day I sat down to write this book, I was sitting in the living room typing away on my MacBook Pro. The 1991 movie *My Girl* was on the TV a few feet away. Now, catching back up with the exploits of young Vada Sultenfuss wasn't my first choice in Netflix films for a lazy Saturday. But my wife, Leslie, wasn't going to get talked out of it. And who was I to argue? It wasn't like I was listening.

But one scene caught my attention as I typed. A teacher named Mr. Bixler is reciting a passage to his adult writing class when eleven-year-old Vada nervously enters from the back of the room. When Mr. Bixler asks why she is there, she says with a sheepish tone that she paid her money for the course. "I wanna be a writer," Vada says. Confused, Mr. Bixler explains that this class is for adults and that she probably shouldn't be there. But after some prodding from another student, Mr. Bixler welcomes Vada to join.

While Vada wanted to be a writer early in life, I didn't decide that I wanted to write until I was in college. Granted, I had toyed with the idea of writing sci-fi books when I was in middle school, but they all sounded too much like *Star Wars*, and I don't think I ever wrote more than a few chapters. As I got older, it was crystal clear that I wasn't much of a writer. I swear that my high school English teachers went through four or five boxes of red ink pens each time they graded my papers. My grammar was deplorable. I was incapable of being imaginative. I hated reading. That's three cardinal sins of writing broken—all before I reached the age of eighteen.

Now, allow me to fast forward a few years to circa 1996 or 1997. I stood in the hallway just outside my college journalism professor's office. He didn't have a ton of time to talk, but he wanted to go over an article I had written.

His critique was short and harsh: "Have you ever read a newspaper before?"

Everything else he said passed in a blur. Even ten minutes later—long after he had walked away to his next class—I was still fixated on those seven condescending words. *Of course, I had read a newspaper before*, I thought! Okay, so maybe it had been a while since I read an article from start to finish, but I had a general idea.[1] My attempt couldn't have been that bad, could it? Besides, my degree was going to be in broadcast journalism. I didn't need to be Hemingway—just good enough to write a few lines for the teleprompter. Right?

Looking back, I didn't have a clue. And perhaps I wasn't taking the profession as seriously as I should. But still, something kept drawing me back to writing. On top of that, I wouldn't have been able to live with myself for failing at something. So I wised up. I became a student of the craft, always striving to do everything better than I did the day before.

My first real job was as a high school sportswriter for the *Lewisville News*. I was offered that job the summer before my junior year in college, and I loved it. I wrote some fairly good stuff in those early days. I also wrote a few things that were a step below trash. I kept plugging along, and along the way, I learned what quality writing looked like and held myself accountable for everything I put my name on.

Over the next twenty-plus years, I got my degree and regularly wrote for several media outfits. Some of those included the *Dallas Morning News*, Allen Publishing, Murray Media Group, and the *Denton Record-Chronicle*. I read everything I could get my hands on in hopes of learning even the most subtle tips, tricks, and nuances of writing. I also ventured outside of sports writing and wrote anything I could get my hands on. It didn't matter if it was a feature, an investigative piece, a blog, a movie review, a press release, or a story on a mom-and-pop business. If there was a story to tell, I wanted to tell it. In 2014, I started a writing and editing services company called Edit This, and throughout my lengthy career, I've managed to win a few national, state, and local awards.

My old journalism professor, if he's still around, would be proud—I think.[2]

I am sharing all of this with you because, well, I *really* love writing. I'm not a guy who has a passing interest and has never been in your shoes. I'm also not writing a book just to say that I wrote a book. I've stayed up until 3 a.m. night after night, staring hopelessly at a blank computer screen before, suddenly, the words I'd waited so long for finally fit together like magical puzzle pieces. I've agonized over the smallest of errors. I've taken every critique and rejection to heart. I've experienced the riot of emotions many writers face when something they wrote is finally published: *Did people like it? Did they hate it?* I've patted myself on the back *and* questioned if I am good enough—all in the same breath. And I keep coming back for more. I love being a writer!

My goal for this book is simple: to educate. But not in a boring, textbook way. I want to share what I've learned, tell a few down-to-earth stories, and have a real conversation about writing, writers, and how we can master our passion for the written word. I've got quite a bit of practical knowledge in this noggin—either because someone passed it down to me or because I learned it through years of trial and error.

My audience is broad and includes but is not limited to:

- Anyone who wants to be a writer.
- Anyone who knows a writer.
- Anyone who was told they shouldn't be a writer.
- Writers who doubt themselves.
- Anyone who isn't sure if they have the chops to write.
- Writers who have already started but don't know what to do next.
- Veteran writers looking to reinvent themselves.
- High school teachers and college professors who teach writing.
- Teachers and professors who want to get inside the mind of a writer.
- Any writer who just wants to hear from another writer.
- Anyone who takes the time to read this book.

Regardless of where you are on your writing journey, I hope this book reaffirms your passion for writing and gives you the tools to *write like you mean it*—whatever that may look like for you. I genuinely believe that being a writer is the greatest job in the world. And if you've read this far, I know you think that, too.

Start Writing!

1

Don't Be Afraid to Write!

"Even the greatest was once a beginner.
Don't be afraid to take that first step."

—Muhammad Ali

I believe the hardest part about getting started as a writer is getting out of our own way. Specifically, overcoming our fears. I mean, think about it: fear affects almost every writer at one time or another. It could be the young Vada Sultenfuss who craves acceptance in a room full of adult writers or the veteran who knows all the tricks of the trade but refuses to call themselves an accomplished writer. I'm the latter in that sentence. Even after more than twenty years of quality storytelling, it still makes my stomach flip end over end almost every time I submit something for publication or turn something over to a client for approval. That includes this book. Don't get me wrong. I'm proud of this book and everything it offers to writers. I'm also petrified that you won't pull something valuable from it and that it will flop.

The struggle is real for many of us. The trick is not to allow these fears and insecurities to be so debilitating that they keep me—or you—from pursuing our passion. At some point, we must believe in ourselves and be confident in our work. We also have to be both gracious and thick-skinned enough to accept what people say or think about our work. So naturally, I figured the best place to start a book for writers is by getting our fears out in the open and then dissecting them so that, hopefully, we can overcome them together. So let's dive right in.

While there is some overlap, I believe there are two types of fears writers face:

1. Fear of writing.
2. Fear of what others will think.

Fear of Writing

Writers afraid of writing just seems weird. Why would anyone fear something that is their passion? We should all be eager to sit down and knock out a few chapters of a book on a rainy weekend or show our personality through poetry, blogs, feature writing, or other creative writing. We should also be eager to share our creation with the world! Instead, paradoxical as it might seem, many of us keep our talents hidden. In many writers' minds, writing is more of a hobby than a potential career. Many individuals who could be published continually second-guess their places at the proverbial writer's table, and many published writers have tens of thousands of words that never see the light of day. We writers agonize, overedit, create excuses, and run the risk of never finishing what we start.

To illustrate my point, let's talk about my wife. Leslie and I have been married for years, and besides being a loving wife and doting mother,

Leslie has always been an incredibly talented baker and cook. I weighed 165 pounds when we first met, and I swear that she made it her mission in life to fatten me up with delicious five-star meals and delectable treats fit for a king. Needless to say, I'm not complaining. Whether she's prepared cupcakes, cookies, or a smash cake for a baby's first birthday party, my wife can make your sweet tooth grow a pair of arms and do cartwheels in your mouth. For years, I told her she needed to start a business. But she never would. "It's just a hobby," she'd say. "There are plenty of real bakers out there. I'm just a mom who likes to cook and make a few treats every once in a while."

Leslie has a talent and a passion for baking, but despite this, for many years, she lacked confidence in her potential—even with something she loved to do. It wasn't until she got opportunities to bake for a couple of my friends that she realized just how talented she is and that she doesn't have to be fearful of, well, anything. And now, she has a successful home baking business.

In the same way my wife feared dismissal, we writers can be fearful that, despite our deep love for the craft, the wider world will just see us as enthusiasts. I mentioned earlier that I tried writing a few sci-fi books when I was younger but never finished. I now realize it wasn't because I didn't have the desire to do it. I was afraid. I didn't think I was good enough. Who was I to think I could be a writer? So I quit before I started and used the fact that it sounded too much like *Star Wars* as an excuse not to challenge myself. I remember showing an excerpt to my dad one night, and he said it was fantastic and to keep going. But I didn't. So here I am, writing my first book in my forties. This type of fear happens more often than you think for a lot of writers, even those you look up to and want to emulate.

Fear of What Others Will Think

Beyond the fear of being dismissed as amateurs and having our love for the craft thrown back in our faces before anyone ever reads a word, many aspiring writers have a secondary fear of *sharing* their work—having it published and potentially read by hundreds of thousands of people—and subsequently judged. Even if we don't necessarily fear the act of writing poetry, song lyrics, blogs, newspaper articles, or novels, we hold back out of fear of what people will say or think, how they'll react, and what type of feedback they'll give.

"What if they find a mistake?" we worry.

"Will they call me a fraud?"

"Am I ready for what people might say about this?"

It's like the movie *Back to the Future*, where Marty McFly travels back in time to 1955 and ultimately runs into his parents. There's a scene between Marty and his teenage father, George, in the high school cafeteria that illustrates this exact fear. Marty is trying to convince George to ask Lorraine out for a date when he gets sidetracked. George is barely listening as he feverishly writes in a notebook. When Marty asks George what he's doing, he is shocked to find out that George loves to write sci-fi stories. Marty reaches across the table to see if he can read some of it, but George stops him and insists that he never lets anyone read his stories. When Marty asks why, George says, "Well, what if they didn't like them? What if they told me I was no good? I guess that would be pretty hard for somebody to understand."

I can't blame anyone for struggling with this aspect of fear. There is an incredible amount of vulnerability that comes with writing something and then putting it out there for the masses. After all, we're also putting a piece of ourselves out there.

I felt paralyzed by this fear for a long time. Maybe not quite to the same extent as George McFly, but it was a struggle for me. And to be totally transparent, it still is in a lot of respects. My voice cracked and shook when I made the initial call to the publishing company about this book. When they said to send them my manuscript, I hesitated for a good thirty minutes before pulling the trigger. During the week or so that I waited for them to get back to me . . . well, let's just say I wondered heavily if they'd bother to read the entire thing before rejecting it. I was convinced they'd reject it, even though I thought this was a very helpful book that needed to be published.

The good news is that I've worked extremely hard over the years to quit looking at feedback and possible rejection as a negative. And with the exception of a few lapses, I've come a long way.

I remember getting an email from a reader a few years ago who said that they loved my writing but felt compelled to point out an error in one of my blogs. The post focused on why you don't use apostrophes to pluralize last names. (Example: It's not *Merry Christmas from the Gamel's*. It's *Merry Christmas from the Gamels*). It drives me up a wall when I see this mistake on holiday cards! Somehow, I goofed up one of my examples by making the same mistake I had preached to others that they must not make under any circumstances. Ugh! Massive fail on my part! The reader joked and said, "I was about to give you an 'atta boy' until . . ." It turned out to be a fun exchange, though, and one that I completely welcomed. That same day, I received a Facebook message from a friend about a typo in another blog. Not only did I correct the errors, but I thanked both readers for saving me from future embarrassment.[1] I've had some really good conversations with people who loved my work. I've had others where they didn't like it. But I've learned to embrace them all the same.

All writers should be less fearful of what may or may not happen and instead embrace situations where readers, publishers, and critics alike have something to say—good, bad, or indifferent. Here's why:

1. Creating a space for feedback opens up lines of communication.
2. Readers who find mistakes know you aren't perfect! That makes you relatable and occasionally even more marketable.
3. When readers and critics reach out, you have a better indication of who your readers are.
4. When you receive feedback, you learn to deal with your fears in a constructive way.
5. You become more aware of your strengths and weaknesses.
6. You become a more effective writer.

I don't know many writers who aren't a little fearful and wouldn't like to be better at what they do every day. My sister-in-law once told me, "I hate it when I spend tons of time working hard on a piece only to find that I've missed a super important detail, it's completely unclear, or what I've written is complete garbage."[2] She's right! Becoming a better writer is a lifelong process. And it's personal. We want to inspire readers and ourselves. It's okay to care and be a little fearful—but not at the expense of your passion. As writers, sharing our work is the only way to keep growing.

Getting Past the Fear

So how do you overcome your fears about writing? I'm sure the easy answer for the snarky writers out there who have never experienced these fears would be: "Just stop caring about what others think!" But that's easier said than done. Here are a few easy tips for overcoming that desire to shrink when you feel you might be dismissed as an amateur or because of what others might say about your writing. These tips are a great starting point, and it would behoove you to put at least a few into practice.

Embrace your fears. Being fearful isn't all bad. In fact, I've come to learn that fear shows you really care about doing well. Think about it: if you didn't care about your writing and lacked emotional investment in some way, the end product probably wouldn't be that good. Fear can motivate you to churn out quality content.

Believe in your ability to write. Sylvia Plath said, "The worst enemy to creativity is self-doubt." You owe it to yourself to build your self-confidence and believe that you are talented. Stop telling yourself that you're a terrible writer. Tell yourself that you are a fantastic writer. Even if it isn't true right now, if you put the time and work into it, it will be eventually! When you flip the script and start telling yourself you *can* instead of *can't*, you'll see five things start to happen more and more:

1. You'll start to *think* you can.
2. That confidence will show up in your writing.
3. You'll write more often.
4. You'll improve as a writer.
5. You'll grow eager to share your writing with the masses.

Stop worrying too much about what others think. The snarkers do have a point: you can't please everyone. Some people will love everything you write. Some will hate it or question every choice you made. Others might be so indifferent that they won't bother to read it at all. Of course, you want readers to love *and* read your work, but at the end of the day, people will think what they want to think. And that's okay. When you view what people think as negative so much that you stop writing altogether, it becomes your problem more than theirs. At the end of the day, remember: you write for yourself.

Accept criticism as an opportunity for growth. It used to bug me when readers critiqued my writing. Who am I kidding? It still bugs me—even if just a little bit. I want my writing to be perfect, and I want to crawl into a hole when it's not. But nobody's perfect, so nothing anyone creates is perfect either. It helped me when I began thinking of critiques this way: if people are critiquing my writing or voicing their opinions, that means they are reading it. Furthermore, if they are taking the time to shoot me a text or email, that means they probably have a vested interest in what I'm writing. When you look at it like that, criticism can be a good thing. When you receive it, look at it as an opportunity for growth.

Become an expert. If you want to be a more effective writer and overcome your initial fears, one great way to get there is to do everything you can to expand your knowledge. Sign up for a few writer's workshops and read what others have said, written, or researched about the topics or type of writing you enjoy. Formulate your own opinion. The more comfortable and knowledgeable you are, the less insecure you'll be.

Ask someone you trust to read your writing. If you want to know what someone thinks of your writing before taking the plunge and attempting to publish, ask a close friend to take a look and offer feedback. These people are your built-in safety net, and their critiques provide a soft landing as you build momentum. I lost count of the number of friends and mentors I shared this book with, all so I could find out if I was on the right track or if I needed to delete and start all over.

Build yourself a writer's community. The best people to call on who will understand all of your insecurities and offer just the right level of encouragement are—you guessed it—other writers. They could be mentors, classmates, coworkers, and even writers you've always been a tad shy to reach out to in the past. A fellow writer can be a source of compassion and constructive criticism and can provide tips of the trade to help you maintain perspective.

Remember why you do this. Writing is supposed to be fun. It's not open-heart surgery, though it can admittedly feel that way when the words don't quite flow the way you expected them to flow. But that's not enough to make me forget why I do this. Heck, I quit a job as a banker to do this writing gig full time. I knew writing was my passion. It's what I have fun doing. I'm doing what I love. If you feel the same way about writing as I do, when fears and insecurities strike, remember why it's worth it.

I'm not going to convince you that being a writer isn't scary or difficult. As writers, we pour our heart and soul into every character we type, and the mere act of doing that can be scary. Then, when we put the finished product on a giant stage for the world to see, it can dredge up even more fears. The key is to believe in your writing and never let those fears pull the rug out from underneath you and your career.

You are talented. Invest in yourself, overcome your fears, and then get to writing!

2

The Aspiring Writer's Checklist

"Read, read, read. Read everything—trash, classics, good
and bad, and see how they do it. Just like a carpenter
who works as an apprentice and studies the master.
Read! You'll absorb it. Then write. If it's good, you'll
find out. If it's not, throw it out of the window."

—William Faulkner

Sometimes, I wish I could have a mulligan when it comes to how my career has progressed. Don't get me wrong. I wouldn't change a thing about where I've been, what I've accomplished, who I've been able to learn from, the stories I've told, the accolades, etc. I just wish I could have gotten my act together and figured it out faster.

I alluded to this already, but my journey to becoming a professional writer wasn't a straight line. I went to college to be a broadcast journalist, and I didn't even make that decision official until I was already there.

Believe it or not, I also entertained the idea of being an actor. But I figured broadcasting was the logical step. Growing up, I used to stay up until all hours of the night watching guys like Chris Berman and the late Stuart Scott break down all of the day's action on *SportsCenter*. Those guys were like gods to me. They were true wordsmiths; they just did it on television. I loved their catchphrases ("Boo-yah!" and "Back, back, back, back, back" were personal favorites), the quips, the jokes, and, oh . . . the nicknames Berman gave some of the best players in the world (Rollie "Chicken" Fingers, Mike "Pepperoni" Piazza, and Chuck "New Kids on the" Knoblauch).

Berman and Scott had personality and unbridled enthusiasm, and they brought those unique talents to each newscast. Really, the entire crew at ESPN shared the same passion—and still does! Naturally, I thought I could follow in their footsteps. But here's the problem: I didn't have a clue on how to make that dream a reality. And I certainly wasn't "walking the walk" of someone who had those aspirations. I never practiced in front of my bathroom mirror or during car rides to school. I wasn't researching the right colleges an aspiring sportscaster should attend. I didn't look for broadcasting internships. I didn't have a broadcasting mentor going out of their way to whisper words of wisdom in my ear, and I wasn't looking for one either. Few of my friends had similar interests. All the telltale signs that scream, "Hey! This kid really wants to pursue this dream," didn't exist.

Perhaps even more blasphemous was that my high school had its own student-run television station, and in four years, I can't remember if I ever stepped foot in the door. You'd think that would have been a perfect place to get hands-on experience and to see if being a sportscaster was what I really wanted to do with my life. Instead, I just winged it and figured everything career-wise would work itself out.

Luckily, it did. But the long and winding road to realizing my real passion was only beginning. Right out of high school, I went to Northeastern University in Boston (my dad's alma mater). It was a great university, and I made plenty of really good friends. But I missed Texas too much, and I got increasingly homesick the more I thought about it. I spent one semester in Beantown before transferring to the University of North Texas for the spring semester in 1996.

I spent the next three and a half years at UNT as a broadcast journalism student, and a huge chunk of that degree involved learning how to write for print. Early on, I was doing small things for the *North Texas Daily* but don't remember being particularly good at it—hence my journalism professor's comment that I mentioned earlier. Not long after that, I overheard a conversation between a couple of editors in the newsroom; in a nutshell, they both were complaining about me and how bad I was. Despite this, my name was tossed around for a writing opportunity nearby, and during the summer before my junior year in college, I was offered a job as a sportswriter at the *Lewisville News*. I'd be covering the high school sportswriter beat along with laying out pages and coordinating with photographers. That's when things started to take off. While at the newspaper, I interned at Fox 4 in Dallas, did a few radio bits at the university, and even freelanced for a few public TV stations (I still have an old VHS tape with my best work on it). I was still committed to becoming a sportscaster, but as time went on, the idea of following in Berman and Scott's footsteps became less important to me. I suddenly found that I enjoyed writing about sports, and I did it long enough that I became the sports editor and developed a decent following at the schools I was covering. The kids went so far as to nickname me "Newspaper Steve," and pretty soon, coaches, parents, and even my coworkers followed suit. I remember not being sure what to think about the moniker at first, but it grew on me. In fact, if you do enough research, you'll see that I use the same name for my Twitter handle. So, clearly, it stuck.

I had found something that I not only was getting better at but also had a passion for. While some of my friends were going to class, partying, sleeping in on the weekends, and holding down odd jobs, I was juggling my class schedule with being a beat reporter and covering games on Tuesday and Friday nights. Every day was an opportunity to improve, and I seized those moments. Around 2001, the *Lewisville News* was one of several DFW community papers absorbed by the *Dallas Morning News,* and I found myself invested in a long-term career as a writer.

People often ask me if I ever regret not making it on *SportsCenter,* and the answer is no. Quite simply, if it meant that much to me, I would have done a lot more to make sure that dream became a reality. In my mind, I was always meant to be a writer because I chased it and expected only the best from myself. I just didn't realize that was my path until much later in life.

If writing is your passion and you have overcome your fears about stepping into that wider world, you should equip yourself with the necessary tools to be successful and live out that passion for as long as you want. I want to be that voice in your ear offering practical tips that work—a voice that I didn't have growing up but could have had if I asked or turned over enough stones. In this day and age, there is no room for winging it or guesswork if you want to excel as a writer. There are resources all around you, and if you've picked up this book, you're obviously serious about taking the next step.

If you're in high school or college and planted your sights on being a writer, do the following right now.

Interview veteran writers. Grab the bull by the horns. Call, email, or send a questionnaire to a few veteran writers at nearby newspapers and magazines to see if they have time to let you pick their brains. You can do the same with novelists, bloggers, freelance writers, poets, etc. Even if it's just a thirty-minute conversation over a cup of coffee, there are priceless educational and growth opportunities available to you if you're willing to ask. Assuming they are gracious enough to spend some time with you, it's your job to open your heart and be willing to listen and put their advice into practice. I have been asked numerous times to meet up with and mentor aspiring writers, and it has always been my honor to share what I know—and even where I've failed and had to pick myself back up—so that they can get to where they need to be faster. Not everyone will give the best advice. But remember, these are people who have been around the block a time or two. So listen, ask follow-up questions, and incorporate what works for you.

Check out what your school has to offer. Granted, this piece of advice may not apply to everyone. But many high schools have journalism programs, yearbook committees, and elective creative writing courses that can help you dip your toes in the water and even create opportunities to be noticed by larger media outlets. Colleges typically have a university newspaper and various other resources for aspiring writers. It's also essential to trust in your teachers and look at them as more than someone who just writes on a chalkboard and doles out assignments. The odds are high that they have been in the writing or media business before and know important people. Take what they say to heart. This is an opportunity to learn from someone who has been there.

Sign up for additional writing classes. When Vada Sultenfuss realized she wanted to develop as a writer, she signed up for a writing course. Whether it's an elective in high school, a core class in college, or a writing workshop at the local library, there are plenty of online and in-person courses to flex your writing muscles, expand your creativity, share your work, and learn the mechanics of writing. Don't be afraid; others in these classes are in the same shoes you are. If they aren't, they used to be.

Get an internship or summer writing job. There are plenty of writers who started as high school or college interns at major metropolitan newspapers. Some of them do so well that they are immediately hired full time (the college-aged ones, anyway). The point is, there are plenty of organizations that would gladly take you under their wing for a summer. Even freelance writers and novelists wouldn't mind sharing their knowledge and giving you opportunities to learn on the job with smaller assignments that lighten their workload. There is no telling where the opportunity could lead if you get your foot in the door.

Get your portfolio ready. People want to see and read what you've written or edited and projects you've collaborated on—especially if they've made it into print. Make sure your portfolio of writing speaks to your style and experience and shows your range as a budding writer. I remember putting my first portfolio together after I was already a few years into working at the *Lewisville News*. In those days, portfolios weren't digital, so I was literally taking the time to go into the paper's archives, picking the articles I felt best represented my work, and then cutting them out to paste into the binder I had created. I think I also included basic Word documents of creative stuff I had written on the side. I must have worked on that portfolio for three or four weeks, just to make sure it looked perfect. I argued with myself over what should be included and what shouldn't, and I lost a lot of sleep worrying about what hiring editors would say when they read through it. But it was a great exercise, and it helped me get my work in front of some great people. These days, it's a lot easier to show off your work and make it sharable through direct links or portfolio tabs on your own personal website. You won't have to invest the same tedious time into it that I did back in the day. But it's still important to invest some thought into how you want it to look. One tip is to break up your portfolio by category (sports, hard news, poetry, blogs, website copy, etc.) so it has some sort of structure to it.

Expand your writing range. Don't be a one-trick pony—at least not early on in your career. Use your extra time writing about topics that are a tad outside your comfort zone. This is the best way to show someone your work ethic and how valuable you can be to their organization. In 2014, I was freelancing for a local magazine that was only using me for sports writing at the time. Well, one day, they had a new business client (a cake store) purchase an ad at the last minute. That ad came with a three-hundred-word spotlight article. The only problem is that they didn't have anyone available to interview the business owner, write the article, get it approved by the client, and turn it in by the next day. They asked me, and without hesitating, I jumped at it. Not only did it turn out to be a great piece, but the business owner told the powers that be that she couldn't have been happier with the article and that it truly captured the essence of her bakery. I crossed the barrier to become more than just the sports guy at work, and in the future, I had more writing opportunities because of it.

Read with a critical eye. People say that all writers need to read, read, read. While the importance of this cannot be overstated, it is also crucial for writers to read with a critical eye. When you read work by other writers, take some time to think. What did you like or dislike about what you read? How would you have written it differently? Something that irks the heck out of me is when I read something online, and the author takes what feels like a million years to get to the point. It could be an article on ten reasons why sleeping on your stomach at night isn't good for you, and they'll waste my time with eight to nine hundred words of fluff that forces me to scroll several pages down before I finally get to read what I came for. That's not to suggest that there aren't situations in writing where there needs to be a build-up in the action. But with some kinds of writing, getting to the point quickly is the goal. Other kinds of writing have other goals. You'll pick up on them if you take the time to read enough content. Read published work from anyone and everyone. You will learn something from all of them and eventually be able to recognize what quality writing looks like and how to emulate it.

Learn how to fact-check everything. This tip cannot be overstated, especially if you intend to be a journalist. But it's just as important for all writers. Yes, I'm talking to the bloggers out there, as well as the men and women writing copy for company websites or putting out informative social media posts. If you're a student, I'm even talking to you and that term paper you need to write by tomorrow. In today's world, misinformation, unverified facts, false claims, and even plagiarism are rampant—so much so that it's difficult to decipher between original work, fake news, and what's actually true. Be fair in your writing by telling all sides of the story. Ask the right questions, use verifiable research and sources, quote accurately and not out of context, keep your opinion out of it, and get the facts straight—even if it means you aren't the first to break the news. More often than not, journalists are more concerned with being the first to report something than being accurate. And that mindset has given the press—and, really, all writers—a bad name. Actor Denzel Washington once spoke on this, asking the media, "So what a responsibility you all have. To tell the truth—not just to be first. But to tell the truth. We live in a society now where it's just first. Who cares? Get it out there! We don't care who it hurts. We don't care who we destroy. We don't care if it's true. Just say it—sell it."

I have been the first to report on things, and I've also been the last. I've even been the victim of plagiarism a time or two. But I can say unequivocally that I am always accurate and truthful in anything I write. You'll always be able to look yourself in the mirror if you follow that same mindset. And morality aside, well-researched writing that is fact-checked and verified stands out from the horde of fluff and fake news—or historically inaccurate romance novels, for that matter. Doing your homework gives you credibility as a writer and makes your work stronger.

Find your happy place. Self-evaluate and discover what works for you as a writer. What time of day are you most productive? Where do you prefer to write? A nearby coffee shop? A favorite park bench? Your home office? The library? Writing where you are happy and motivated is crucial. For example, I love having my home office. But I love the freedom of moving around and writing from different locations. Sometimes, I'll start the day in my office, and when I feel a little "heavy" and need a change, I'll pack up my laptop and hit the nearest coffee shop. I couldn't do that when the coronavirus hit in March 2020. My first thought was, "Okay, I've still got my home office." Two or three weeks in, though, I was tired of the home office. On top of that, my wife was working from home, and we were homeschooling our kids. I found myself in an emotional and creative rut—and limited on time. So I returned to my self-evaluation methods and looked for different ways to switch things up. I went from being a night owl, writing some of my bigger projects between the hours of 10 p.m. and 3 a.m., to being an early bird and working between 5 and 8 a.m. My space didn't change, but mentally, I didn't feel confined by my surroundings. That's not to suggest doing the same thing during a pandemic or other life circumstances will make a monumental impact on your motivation and creativity. Perhaps you struggle to get your brain working during either of those times. If that's the case, perhaps taking a step back to make peace with what's going on around you will help settle nerves and get you back to writing. I've also found that writing out your feelings, especially in difficult times, helps immensely. I share all of this because small variations in your approach can help with your motivation, creativity, and overall sense of having control over doing your best work.

Don't forget what your own journey has taught you. In 2003— roughly six years after I had realized that writing was my true passion—I lost my job at the *Dallas Morning News*. The *DMN* had purchased several small community newspapers, including the *Lewisville News*, around 2001. At the time that I lost my job, I was roughly twenty-seven years old and struggled to get anyone to give me a chance of working full time in the profession. After exhausting all my resources, I decided to get into banking, where my girlfriend and eventual wife was working. I was in the banking world for ten years, working my way up from a teller to a branch manager. I did freelance writing work any chance I could get, juggling my full-time job with covering games at night, doing movie reviews, writing features, and taking on other assignments. There were countless days where I'd work 8 a.m. to 5 p.m. at the bank and then hightail it to the other side of the city to cover a game that started at 7 p.m. I'd work until 11 p.m. or midnight, and then do it all over again the next day. There were other days where I'd get up early to write a feature story, then go to the bank all day. I'd even squeeze in other articles that needed to be written during my hour lunch break. That may sound like torture to some people, but I loved it. In fact, I couldn't get enough of it—to the point where I was constantly looking for ways to do it full time again. I eventually took a massive leap of faith by quitting the banking world to start Edit This. Though that time in my life was a detour that I didn't expect, it taught me a lot. I learned how to talk to people, run a business, problem-solve, and, among other things, how to multitask and be willing to embrace situations that were previously outside my comfort zone. I also learned how far I was willing to go to chase my passion for a living. My journey wasn't ideal, but I never forgot what it taught me—and I'd like to think I'm a better writer and business owner because of it.

How to Keep Writing When You're Sick

If you have a laundry list of projects to keep up with, giving up even one or two days of productivity isn't always in the cards. So how do you keep writing while you're sick?

- **Pace yourself.** Pace yourself with shorter bursts of creativity rather than powering through five to six hours at a time.

- **Switch up your surroundings.** When you're sick, you may not be able to go into the office. Take your laptop to bed or write out in the fresh air on the patio.
- **Keep everything you need close.** Keep all tissues, medications, and beverages right by your workstation. This gives you every reason to stay exactly where you are and write.
- **Be okay with slow and steady.** When you're feeling good, it's easy to work faster. When you're writing while you're sick, your . . . brain . . . moves . . . slower. Prepare yourself, knowing that something that typically takes an hour to write may take double or triple that time.[3]

How Writers Can Organize the Writing Process

Once you have put yourself in a position to chase your passion for writing, it's time to focus on ways you can improve your writing habits. At the top of that list is improving your ability to organize the writing process.

This is one area where many writers, including yours truly, feel like they are drinking from a gushing firehose. How many of you have faced this scenario? You have several notes in one notepad, a few more spread out over several sticky notes or cocktail napkins, and even more on a few pieces of loose paper at the office. On top of that, there are interview notes and quotes you have transcribed on your computer, notes in your phone, voice recordings and reminders to your future self, additional thoughts still floating around in your head, etc. It's a lot of great stuff—but it's also a giant mess. When you finally do sit down to write, you're not sure where to start or which end is up.

There are plenty of strategies for writers looking to untangle the web of creativity and get organized. And what works best for one may not benefit another. But next time you sit down to craft your next blog, book, poem, article, dissertation, etc., try doing this:

Go to your laptop and turn it on. Open a separate Word document (not the one you plan to use for your formal piece).

Pool together all relevant information for your project. By that, I mean transcribe any notes or interviews you have saved on a recorder or written in shorthand on a notepad or Post-it Note. Convert any story shells or outlines from any other handwritten sources as well. Get everything written down in one place. Once you have done this, you can go a step further and start grouping related elements or thoughts together through a simple cut and paste to create a flow—especially if you see obvious groupings.

When you're done transcribing, freewrite your raw thoughts into an outline or story shell—in the same document. When I say "freewrite," I mean write whatever immediately springs to mind without worrying about punctuation, grammar, spelling, or style. Too often, writers want everything to be perfect the first time. Freewriting allows a writer to be creative and less constrained by rules.

What you have done in three simple steps is organize the writing process. It may still be a lot of information, but at least it's in one document. There's no need to refer to your notepad, listen to a recording, or plan as you write—it's all mapped out in front of you.[1]

But you're not done yet. One thing I like to do after this discovery and organization stage is to take a break and let everything "marinate" in my mind. I give myself time to process what I've done so far and take a deep breath before jumping into formal writing. This break could be thirty minutes, an hour, or even a few hours later (if I have time to wait that long). I'll then sit down, pull that "notes" document over to the far right of my computer screen, and open a fresh document to the left. This places two documents side by side. The one on the right has all of my notes. The one on the left is where I'll write my article. If you really want to get techy, use a dual-monitor setup.

Writing is a creative thing. Generally, most creative types are scattered and have ideas and notes all over the place. I'm no different in a lot of respects. But I've also learned from plenty of my writing projects that the more I organize the process and get everything into its rightful place (or as close to it as possible), the less stressed I am, and the easier it is to see the story in my head.

As you organize your thoughts, you may find you also need to organize your space. Think about what kind of tools you use to write. Some people might think all a writer needs is a laptop, a notepad, a pen, and plenty of coffee. Those certainly are important, but there are plenty of additional tools that can make everything easier. From office and desk tools to go-to resources and phone apps, there are so many essentials every writer needs at their fingertips to help them work efficiently, stay organized, block distractions, and make sure their writing always sounds good. Consider how some of the following might help your work.

Lap desk. Obviously, you want to use a desk or table to write your best stuff, but sometimes writers find themselves typing away on the couch, in bed, or as a passenger on a long car ride. Lap desks are great for making these situations a bit more comfortable. I got mine from Best Buy a few years ago, and it has really come in handy during long car rides or if I want to switch up my surroundings. A few years ago, the wife, kids, and I packed ourselves into a Suburban with my parents and drove from Houston to Santa Rosa Beach in Florida. We took turns driving, but when I wasn't behind the wheel, I had my lap desk out and was typing away on several writing projects.

Voice and call recorder. There are free phone apps you can use to record calls and interviews. When you implement them into your routine, it means no more shorthand note taking, no more asking the person on the other line to repeat what they said, and no more wondering if you got the quote right. One note: If you use voice recorders to record a client or source for an article, it's probably a good idea to let them know. You don't want to get in trouble for recording anything without someone's permission.

***The Chicago Manual of Style* and the *AP Stylebook*.** Stylebooks and style manuals are tremendous resources for those of us who spend our days trying to figure out the English language. Which one to use depends on you or the organization you're writing for. *The Chicago Manual of Style* is used by editors, authors, and publishers of books, etc., while the *AP Stylebook* is for those writers and editors in the newspaper and public relations world. If you're working for a company that has an internal style for any written content or marketing materials, make sure you have that handy. Likewise, use whatever style or formatting your professors require.

Standing desks. There are so many compact standing desk solutions out there. I use a simple laptop version through Varidesk. There are also cushioned standing pads out there that make a world of difference from standing on a hard floor all day. Standing desks and cushioned floors aren't a necessity for writing. But they are luxuries that I've found improve my posture and help me keep plugging along when I'm tired of sitting around all day.

Evernote or another note-taking app. Stay organized and jot down those notes and ideas while you're on the move with apps like Evernote. This is perfect for the techies of the world. I can't tell you how many times I've been in a meeting or sitting in a waiting room or at a stoplight and had inspiration strike. Along with using a pen and pad of paper, being able to pull out my phone and keep track of everything has saved me on more than one occasion. There have even been a few times that I've written a shell for a blog using the notes app on my phone.

Aqua Notes. Imagine standing in the shower and needing to write something down. Using your finger to jot notes on the steamy glass isn't practical, so someone way smarter than all of us created waterproof notepads that come complete with suction cups for the shower wall and a waterproof pencil. As they say, you will never lose another great idea. I believe in this product so much that I regularly buy them in bulk and use them as giveaways at various networking events, mixers, or speaking events. People love them.

Noise-canceling headphones. Headphones are a great tool for minimizing distractions and improving concentration—though sometimes it can feel that the "noise-canceling" or "noise-isolating" monikers are a stretch, depending on your surroundings. Still, if you do most of your writing in a loud newsroom, busy coffeehouse, or in a home office that sometimes doubles as your kids' play area, headphones might be a good investment. I use Beats by Dr. Dre, but there are many other brands.

Grammarly. This online grammar checker is well worth the yearly fee because everyone needs an extra set of eyes on what they write. Grammarly doesn't just correct basic spelling mistakes. It also improves your writing by picking up on improper word placement, missing commas, too much use of the passive voice, wordy sentences, and various other things you might never catch on your own. Install it on any computer or on your phone.

Transcription software. The downside of using digital voice recorders or smartphone call recorders is that you may have tons of transcription to do afterward. Transcription software does it all for you. This makes for a more efficient and organized writer. Sometimes writers may be unable to afford it. If that's true for you, don't be too discouraged. Many writers look negatively upon manually having to transcribe notes, but going through this tedious process manually has often allowed me to collect my thoughts and improve my organization skills—even if it occasionally takes a really long time.

External hard drive. This is definitely one of those essentials every writer needs. Anyone who owns a computer needs an external hard drive, especially if you have sensitive material such as family photos and important files or documents. It's a writer's worst nightmare to lose everything when a computer decides to die. Saving backups to the virtual cloud is one way to preserve your work, but a solution that works even when the Wi-Fi's out is always better. For that reason, I back up all my documents on my external hard drive.

Google calendar. If you are not using a calendar to manage your time as a writer or as a student who wants to be a writer—especially if you have several projects going on at the same time—then you are doing yourself and potential clients a disservice. Some people prefer the big desk calendars or physical day planners that they can carry with them. My calendar is on my phone, and I update it every day to avoid any potential conflicts or missed assignments.[2]

With dedication, the right strategies, and even better writing tools by your side, your dreams of being a writer will become a reality. I can't stress enough how important it is to put in the work early and chase down everything that will aid you in being a better writer. Reach out to other writers, especially those who are in the area of writing you plan to pursue. Immerse yourself in writing courses, internships, and other opportunities to perfect your craft. Read—a lot! Write as much as you can on as much as you can. And make the writing process easier on yourself rather than more stressful. You'll be a better writer because of it.

3

Active Voice and Mechanics: Simple Ways to Improve Your Writing

"I notice that you use plain, simple language, short words and brief sentences. That is the way to write English—it is the modern way and the best way. Stick to it; don't let fluff and flowers and verbosity creep in."

—Mark Twain, Letter to D. W. Bowser

One of the best writers I've met, and someone I have the utmost respect for, is the gentleman I asked to pen the foreword for this book. Scott Parks is the epitome of an old-school newspaper guy. Shortly after graduating college, he worked at the *Denton Record-Chronicle* before moving on to a paper in Wichita Falls and then another in Corpus Christi. By 1979, he was at the *Dallas Morning News*. During that stretch and well into the years to follow, he wrote countless thought-provoking articles and did his best to shape the standard for quality journalism. He even spent time as a television station news director. No matter how accomplished he became, he never stopped living by the "write like you mean it" philosophy.

I met Scott in 2014 at the tail end of his career when he was back at the *DRC* as the managing editor. I was a freelancer, and they approached me about taking over an open spot in the sports department. I happily accepted, provided that it was okay with them that I continued growing my new company, Edit This, on the side. Scott said it was fine, so long as it didn't interfere with my responsibilities at the paper. I never told Scott this, but he intimidated the hell out of me that day. It wasn't that he was mean or unwelcoming. He was and still is an extremely nice and helpful guy. I just took one look at him—the solid white head of hair, how he studied me, and how every word he chose felt like he carefully designed it in a lab—and quickly decided, *This is one guy I don't want to disappoint.* And it was a good thing that I had that mentality. There was no doubt that Scott expected the best from us. He challenged us as writers and pushed us to think outside the box with thought-provoking investigative journalism that went beyond the typical game coverage on Friday nights. The result was amazing features, investigative projects, and other daily content that netted numerous awards. We gave readers a reason to be excited.

I genuinely felt Scott was someone I could learn from for years down the road. And he rewarded me by never being short on pithy stories, advice, quips, and lessons that helped me become a better writer. One in particular has stuck with me.

"Learning to be a good writer is a roll-up-your-sleeves endeavor," he told me. "It's not easy. It's hard, and it's a lifelong process where you're never really there. But you can learn to do it better and better and better as time goes on by focusing on using the active voice and basic mechanics of writing."

When you commit to becoming the best writer you can be, it's not enough to organize your space so it's conducive to writing and surround yourself with useful tools. You want to improve your writing itself, and one of the easiest and most effective ways to do that is by paying attention to the lessons you probably shrugged off in middle and high school. I fully subscribe to the belief that if you focus on good, clean writing at its basic level—perfect grammar; an active, powerful voice; a varied sentence structure and word choice—the story you're trying to tell falls into place. You eliminate all the riffraff that bogs down your writing and makes your message harder to relay to the reader. Conversely, the reader finds your writing easy and enjoyable to read. They can't wait to flip to the next page. Their focus is only on the information they're reading about.

What Is Writing in the Active Voice?

The mechanics of writing come before story concepts, story organization, narrative devices, or showing versus telling. These are all separate issues. Before a reader can appreciate any of that, they must be able to see words that fit together well on a page. It's like Scott said in his foreword:

> "The writer is like the cabinetmaker who strives to build the perfect chest of drawers. The pieces of wood must fit together seamlessly. The drawers must slide in and out as if they were riding on air."

Part of this is spelling, subject-verb agreement, knowing the difference between "your" and "you're" and "its" and "it's" and the like. But consistently using the active voice is perhaps the simplest and most powerful way to begin to materially strengthen your writing. Just a few benefits of using the active voice include:

1. Your sentences are stronger, more direct, and impactful.
2. You make it clear who in the sentence is acting.
3. The reader feels the emotion of your writing.

With the active voice, the subject in the sentence acts upon its verb. Conversely, using the passive voice takes the opposite approach—the subject receives the action of the verb.

Let's take a look at some examples.

Passive voice: This book was written by me.
Active voice: I wrote this book.

Passive voice: A scathing Facebook post was written by the angry mom.
Active voice: The angry mom wrote a scathing Facebook post.

Passive voice: It was a dreary day in Denton, Texas.
Active voice: Dreariness descended upon Denton, Texas.

Passive voice: The boy was chased by the dog.
Active voice: The dog chased the boy.

Passive voice: Steve was yelled at by Leslie for not doing the laundry.
Active voice: Leslie yelled at Steve for not doing the laundry.

Do you notice how easy it is to read each active voice example in comparison to the passive voice version? I'm willing to bet that you read these five examples and thought, "Yeah. Those passive options are obvious. They seem pretty simple to avoid." Yes. They do! But you'd be surprised how bogged down and less clear our writing becomes when we are knee-deep in a thousand-word article or forty-thousand-word manuscript and are more focused on getting our thoughts down on paper than on the best way to convey them. We forget about the active voice.

Writing in the active voice isn't easy. It ends up being a tedious process, having to analyze every word you write and how they work with the other words you've chosen. As a result, many writers choose to ignore it or occasionally write in the passive voice simply because it's easier to develop a subject more in-depth. And I can't disagree with them. Sometimes, the situation and style of your writing call for passive voice. I've often toed that line to tell a story in a way that makes the most sense. Any eagle-eyed editor will tell you from reading this book that there were several instances of passive voice writing that made it past the final line edits.

And why? Because they worked.

With that said, using the passive voice too much leads to weak writing and dilutes the action in the content. Your reader is forced to slow down. And if they have to slow down too often, they may stop reading. And no one wants that.

Use active voice for the majority of what you write. Your readers will thank you.

Tips to Improve Your Writing

I have experimented with the type of writing I produce. I study the English language like a hawk. My thirst to be a better writer than I was even a day ago is unquenchable. When you are looking for some quick tips to improve your writing, these things might help:

- **Be concise.** Keep your writing simple and get to the point quickly. If you can eliminate words without changing the meaning or tone of a sentence, then do it.
- **Use a conversational style.** There are times to be formal, but in most cases, you should write the same way you speak. It's easier for the reader to understand, and you build rapport and credibility as a writer.
- **Ask for feedback.** Always bounce your content off someone else before going to print. They can ensure you are on the right track and that what you've written is understandable.
- **Avoid using generalities or hasty, unsupported generalizations.** I have always been big on adding facts and figures, doing research, talking to other people, and anything else that will add perspective to my writing.[2]

Shortening Wordy Sentences

As you begin to focus on the mechanics of your writing—the word-by-word makeup of the sentences and paragraphs you compose—you may find that using the active voice is only one way to strengthen your writing. Another is shortening wordy sentences. Wordiness is everywhere in our writing, adding unnecessary padding and fluff that:

1. Makes each sentence less clear.
2. Creates a slower moving narrative.
3. Forces the reader to work harder.

Perhaps you've noticed this in your own writing. You have so much good stuff to write, but it's too wordy when you finish putting pen to paper. You need to cut something. But what? And how?[1] Start by looking back at something you wrote recently. Read it closely. Is there a ten- or twelve-word sentence that could be trimmed to seven or eight without losing its luster? Think of how concise your writing becomes, and how easy it is to read now. Here's one example:

You wrote: "Instead of focusing on all the things that are bad, you have the ability to smile."

But how about: "Instead of focusing on all the bad things, you can smile."

There is a five-word difference between those two sentences, but the five words don't add any value to what was being said. As you look over your writing, you'll be surprised how quickly the unnecessary words add up. Scott always called these "empty calorie" words. Examples like "very," "that," "really," and "more" contribute nothing to your writing and are easy to spot. Here are more examples of inflated wording and their concise counterparts.

You wrote: "At all times . . ."
But how about: "Always"

You wrote: "In light of the fact that . . ."
But how about: "Because"

You wrote: "Have the ability to . . ."
But how about: "Can"

You wrote: "In order to . . ."
But how about: "To"

You wrote: "In the event that . . ."
But how about: "If"

You wrote: "On two separate occasions . . ."
But how about: "Twice"

Shortening wordy sentences has so many applications beyond improving your writing. It can also help you when you're trying to fit a specific space. For example, your teacher asks you to write a 500-word essay. Your finished piece is 532 words, so you need to trim 32 words, right? Or perhaps you're using a newsletter template for your business and need to fit a specific space. With patience and a keen eye, you can shorten practically any sentence and make your writing better because of it.

It's easy to start believing that you're a good writer the longer you do it and the more you start seeing your stuff in print. I want you to start believing that about yourself, but do yourself a favor and never fall into the trap of thinking you've learned everything there is to know about writing. You haven't. You never will, and that's okay. There is always a better way to write something. That's the beauty of being a writer. I am constantly looking back at pieces I wrote three, four, or even five years ago and comparing them to the content I produce now. Trust me, there's a difference. And that isn't to say my writing back then was bad.

I've simply become better at focusing on the basic mechanics of writing—including using the active voice and making sure that every word I use contributes to my point. It usually leads to much better writing.

And tomorrow, I'll be even better at it than I was today.

4

Why a Pen and Paper Are Still Good Tools

"And the idea of just wandering off to a cafe
with a notebook and writing and seeing where
that takes me for a while is just bliss."

—J. K. Rowling

We live in a technology-driven world where it's easy for writers of all types and varying work schedules to sit down with a cup of coffee and a laptop and start typing away about whatever ideas are in our head or whatever topic we need to write for a client. But how many writers still use a pen and paper? Now, let me be clear—I'm not talking about going all stone age and free-handing forty-thousand-word manuscripts or six-hundred-word blogs using nothing but a BIC pen and a spiral notebook with a picture of Darth Vader on the front. That's a ton of hand cramps, if you ask me . . . and way too much transcribing of chicken-scratch notes.

But I maintain there's a lot to be said for using an old-fashioned pen and paper to get those initial creative juices flowing—before you fire up the laptop. Maybe it's to collect a few trivial thoughts that may turn into big elements down the line, jot down an outline, freewrite without worrying about spelling mistakes or missing commas, or—in rare cases—write down a shorter article or even song lyrics that you can perfect later. As Scott Parks said in his foreword, Hank Williams was a genius who could write a perfect song on a cocktail napkin in twenty minutes. While I don't use a pen and paper for everything I do as a writer, the majority of what I've written over the years has been crafted in a notebook first—and yes, sometimes on a napkin. I've blown through thousands of notebooks and notepads over the years because I've found them to be a mighty powerful tool in helping make the writing process easier.

For those who already use a pen and paper, I'm sure this is music to your ears. You may even be saying out loud, "Yes! Finally, someone who gets me!" For those who don't use a pen and paper, hopefully I've got your wheels spinning on how to incorporate them into your writing routine.

Using a pen and paper first will help you as a writer. Here are a few practical reasons why you should incorporate this strategy into your routine.

Writing by hand = happy brain. What did we do before there were computers and smartphones? We wrote everything down. For the older crowd out there, just think about all those spiral notebooks your parents had to buy for you just to get you through half a school year. I love technology, but writing things down forces us to use more of our brain. Writing things down with a pen and paper also improves learning comprehension versus typing it out. It's also very calming.

Surround yourself with notebooks, notepads, sticky notes, and pens and pencils. Keep them on your desk and in your computer bag. You will begin to naturally train your mind to think about writing things down first. Surround yourself with the right tools, and you'll rely on them more often than you think.

You'll never lose those great ideas. Imagine sitting in a waiting room at the doctor's office or mechanic's shop. You're minding your own business and letting your thoughts wander when *boom!* A great opening sentence for your next book hits you like a ton of bricks. This has happened to every writer, and it's annoying because while the idea is almost always amazing, it's also easily lost for good if it's not written down right then and there. Sure, you could just grab your phone, send yourself a text, or write it into a notes app, but I've found it takes too long. The physical piece of handwriting slows you down in a good way. You can put more thought into each word you write, which helps you to get all your ideas out before they vanish into the abyss.

Stow pens and paper in your car, in your pockets, in your purses and bags, on the kitchen counter at home, and in your bedside table. It can help you out tremendously when you aren't near your computer and need to jot something down. There is also Aqua Notes, which I mentioned in a previous chapter. Look it up; it's basically a waterproof pencil and paper pad for when you're in the shower and need to write something down.

You're surprisingly more creative. I'm going to defer to a writer by the name of Lee Rourke on this one because I agree with him 100 percent. In a post for *The Guardian* called "Why Creative Writing is Better with the Pen," Mr. Rourke said, "For me, writing longhand is an utterly personal task where the outer world is closed off, just my thoughts and the movement of my hand across the page to keep me company. The whole process keeps me in touch with the craft of writing. It's a deep-felt, uninterrupted connection between thought and language which technology seems to short circuit once I begin to use it."

Mr. Rourke wondered later in the same piece how many writers still use longhand, and he even suggested that he might be part of a dying breed. I don't think so. I think there are plenty of writers of all experience levels who still use a pen and paper to write some of their most creative work. They just don't share that little nuance. To them, it's just part of what they do. If I weren't writing this book, I probably wouldn't even have shared that side of me. Explore what works for you. Make a point to keep pen and paper around, and you may be surprised by what you produce.

You avoid blank computer screens. You hear all the time about how writers find themselves staring at a blank screen, waiting for even a drop of inspiration. You rarely hear people say the same thing about a blank piece of paper.[1] Studies have shown that writing things down first helps you informally collect your thoughts, as if to suggest, "None of this counts, so just write what you're thinking." When you're in front of the computer screen, that's when your mind is thinking more formally. You may begin to worry, waiting for something brilliant to come to you. When you have a notepad and a pen, the pressure is off. There's not as much of a mental wall—at least not for me.

Before I fire up the laptop, I've made a habit of sitting down for five to ten minutes and writing a few of the key elements I need to build momentum. That could be focusing on the first two or three sentences only or simply focusing on an outline. I also do this if I find that I'm sitting at the computer for too long without making much progress. It helps me reset and ease the pressure of being formal with my writing.

You can stay focused longer. I love my laptop, but it's so easy to get distracted from writing by the internet, email notifications, and friends' social media posts. Last time I checked, your favorite pen and notepad don't have Wi-Fi capability. Use that to your advantage.[2]

If you are finding it difficult to concentrate without getting distracted, go outside on the patio or sit under a tree with only your pen and a notepad. Leave the laptop at home or in your office. And while you're at it, leave your phone, smartwatch, or any other electronic device behind, too. The last time I did this, I was able to handwrite near-perfect copy for a website project in thirty minutes—half the time it had taken me to write the first paragraph using my laptop.

Grammar rules don't exist. I know a lot of people who probably just read that and said out loud, "Sweet! I can live in this space!" In all seriousness, though, I am constantly editing and focusing on grammar as I'm writing on my laptop, which can lead to lost ideas and lost train of thought as I find myself in a start-stop, start-stop, start-stop mode. Using a pen and paper allows me to throw rules out the window and focus on scribing my raw thoughts. Some people call this freewriting. Others say it is writing using a stream of consciousness.

You probably don't need much prodding to write in an unrestricted fashion. I've found that I can breeze through certain projects by using my own form of shorthand, chicken scratch, etc. There are no rules. All you have to do is start writing.

Give pen and paper a try. We all love our laptops and the convenience of technology, but some of the best literary works from yesteryear were crafted with a simple pen and paper. It's the bedrock of what writing is all about. Sure, times have changed, but when you're a writer, you should be looking for every advantage you can get to churn out your best stuff. And sometimes, that means going back to your old-school roots.

5

The Hidden Messages of Writer's Block

"Writer's block is real. It happens. Some days you sit down at the old typewriter, put your fingers on the keys, and nothing pops into your head. Blanko. Nada. El nothingissimo. What you do when this happens is what separates you from the one-of-these-days-I'm-gonna-write-a-book crowd."

—James N. Frey

Sometimes, all the organization in the world is not enough. You can open up a dozen journals and notepads, and the ideas still don't flow. Ugh. Writer's block! The one thing that can take all the great ideas and processes that I've laid out for you so far and make them seem about as fruitful as trying to hammer a nail into a brick with a pencil. Writer's block is that horrible feeling where you stare at a blank computer screen for so long that you swear the blinking cursor is mocking you—or maybe that you'll eventually be buried alive by all the crumpled-up pieces of paper from your notebook. Writer's block strips you of your creative juices, turns your brain into mush, and honestly makes you feel like a horrible writer.[1] There's nothing tangible about it, either. We can't touch it. We can't see it. We can't punch it in the face. Yet we've all experienced it. We've all beaten it only to have it rear its ugly head again and again—and again, seemingly without explanation. Quite frankly, you'd be hard-pressed to find anyone crazy enough to say anything positive about it other than, well . . . ME!

I did a quick search of the internet and found pages upon pages of results with experts offering sage advice on how to beat writer's block forever. It's all good stuff, and I mention several tips throughout this chapter that I hope will work for you. Still, very few of those articles try to find the value in writer's block.

What if I told you that writer's block isn't such a bad thing? Don't get me wrong. I hate writer's block just as much as you do. It's like that bully on the playground who always gave you a wedgie right as you were finally about to talk to the prettiest girl at school. The havoc it creates knows no limits. I get it. But—and I know this is a wild concept here—perhaps it's trying to tell us something. Perhaps it's trying to make us better writers! I believe that in many instances, this is very much the case. I'll even go a step further by suggesting that we often bring writer's block on ourselves.

Before you try to hang me up by my toes, hear me out first. Let's quit pointing fingers at writer's block and focus more on what it is trying to tell us.

Writer's Block May Be Saying We're Moving Too Fast

Whenever I get knocked down by writer's block, it's usually because I'm moving too fast for my own good. Maybe my mind is racing a mile a minute, I haven't given myself enough time to process my thoughts and notes, I haven't researched the topic completely, or I'm simply trying to bang something out quicker than what it should progress. Take this book, for example. At one point very early on, I was telling a dear friend of mine how frustrated I was at how slowly these chapters were coming along. I was making progress, but it was the equivalent of watching the progress bar on my laptop as it tried to download the next software update. All I wanted to do was hit the fast-forward button. What I realized was that the fun part is the journey, and in this case, it was better to slow . . . the heck . . . down. My friend replied, with her trademark eloquence, "How do you eat an elephant? One bite at a time."

You may be thinking, "What about those situations where I am racing to beat a deadline, and there's little time to process?" Well, some of that may be due to time management issues, which I will get to in a little bit. But in instances where you are on a legit deadline, such as for a breaking news story or another writing assignment that requires you to think on your feet, the same rule applies.

In my sportswriter life, I've covered games that didn't finish until 10:15 p.m., and my hard deadline to write a five-hundred-word game story was 10:30 p.m. That can make even the most veteran writers freak out. There are a multitude of ways to help yourself work out of these writer's block jams, but the first step is to mentally slow down and tackle each project sentence by sentence. This helps you reset, get those ideas flowing, and move forward uninhibited. You can slow the writing process—and your brain—down by doing any of the following:

1. Practice a few deep breathing techniques. I like to inhale to the count of four, hold it for two counts, and then exhale for six counts.

2. Allow your mind to relax. Try meditating for one minute. Close your eyes and focus on what you know and what you envision to be the result.

3. Walk away and do something different.

4. Change your scenery. I have several "offices" that I use to reset and slow my brain. Examples are coffee shops, my patio, a park bench somewhere, the passenger seat of my truck, or even writing under a tree.

5. Focus on the present and what you can accomplish now versus later.

We often rush ourselves unnecessarily. A few years ago, I was trying to crank out an article too fast and realized how little I had accomplished. I'd been trying to work for four hours, and it was still just me and a blank computer screen. Oh, the joy of writer's block! I was in pretty deep. Getting over this hurdle was about all I could focus on. But just as I was about to turn my eyelids inside out, my then-five-year-old son, Jackson, quietly walked up to my desk and climbed on my lap.

"Are we going to work on something, Daddy?" he asked.

"No, buddy," I said sadly. "Not now, anyway."

"Well, let's draw a rainbow fish for my teacher," he suggested.

I'm not the drawing type, but how could I say no to that cute face?[2] So I took a break from my writing and played with my kid. As we were drawing and carrying on a conversation, I began to notice that I was more relaxed. My brain was also slowing down to appreciate the bonding moment we were having. As we patiently sat there and continued to color, my mind cleared, and my thoughts came alive.

I lived to write another day! And Jackson's teacher got a rainbow fish out of it![3]

So when in doubt, slow down!

Writer's Block May Be Saying We Have Too Many Distractions

Your latest bout of writer's block could also be telling you that you simply have too many distractions. Too many emails! Too many texts! Too many phone calls, voicemails, meetings, and errands! Too much social media! Distractions can also take the form of a busy working environment (e.g. a noisy newsroom, coffeehouse, classroom, or home) or of personal issues at home. I've found that it is nearly impossible for me to stay focused and avoid writer's block when faced with these distractions. To combat the countless distractions, here's what I do:

1. Commit to answering emails, texts, calls, etc. during certain hours of the day.
2. Put my phone on airplane mode.
3. Turn social media off.
4. Avoid logging into email until I'm done or ready to take a break from writing.
5. Find a quiet place where it's just me and my writing.

Sometimes, when we're trying to eliminate distractions, it can also help to write at night or very early in the morning when things are calm and quiet. A fellow writer recently asked me if I thought getting things like blogs, feature articles, emails, and other intense projects done early in the morning was better than doing the same work late at night or in the middle of the day. The quick answer is that it all depends on the writer.[4] There isn't one time of day that's best for everyone to write, but it is a good idea to write at a time when you won't encounter a lot of distractions. Personally, I've written late at night and loved it. I recently switched to being an early bird. That has its benefits too. Either way, they are both odd-hour scenarios, which I think are critical for any writer to look into. I've tried writing in the middle of the day but often find myself distracted by other responsibilities, phone calls, honey-do lists, or unforeseen additions to my schedule. What usually takes me roughly an hour to craft might instead take me two or three hours if done in the middle of the day. That's not to suggest that happens to me *every* time, but still, if I have my preference, I work on the more difficult pieces during odd hours.[5]

Writer's Block May Be Saying We Need Better Time Management

There's a difference between moving too fast when you don't have to and doing so because you can't manage your time effectively. This is an easy way to find yourself buried in writer's block, and it will gradually affect everything else in your life. The majority of veteran writers might not have this problem; I usually see it more with students and younger writers who are still trying to find their way. If this is you, it's imperative that you start improving your time management skills now while you are still open to new ideas and better ways to do things. One of the things I did when I was younger was talk to my teachers to get advice. I also turned to my fellow classmates and eventually other writers to see what worked for them. When we practice good time management, everything else falls into place. We feel less "blocked."[6] Here are a few ways to give yourself a fighting chance:

Use a calendar. This should be on everyone's time-management list. I record everything using the Google calendar on my phone and have for years. If I know that I have a big project coming up—even if it's not until next month—I work out a time that works best for me and whomever I'm working with and get it on the calendar now. It helps me mentally prepare and eliminate last-minute planning and writing.

Maximize downtime. Time is a precious resource that is often wasted or mismanaged. Take advantage of the time you spend in a waiting room at the doctor's office or at your car's next oil change. There have been countless blogs and articles that I've written while sitting in a waiting room somewhere.

Redefine office hours. I'm repeating this because it's so important for writers everywhere, and we tend to learn by repetition. Writers should take advantage of times during the day or night when their creative juices are at their peak, and there are fewer interruptions. For me, that's not in the middle of the day. I work a lot late at night or very early in the morning for this very reason.

Set a routine. I have a friend who teases me for being a creature of habit. To a degree, he's right. But when it comes to getting stuff done, establishing a routine is a great strategy and helps me avoid writer's block—if for no other reason than the fact that I know mentally that everything is in order.[7] Whatever routine works for you is fine; just stick with it. If your routine gets blown up—and it usually does—refer back to what I said earlier about slowing your brain and hitting the reset button. This will help you make the necessary adjustments to reclaim the moment.

Designate specific days for projects. Fridays tend to be my go-to days for writing shorter blogs for my clients, whereas Sundays are perfect for focusing on long-form writing, research, and other larger projects. Picking specific days to work helps me mentally prepare and avoid the potential for writer's block.

Reevaluate your processes. We all must take a hard look at the strategies we have in place and question whether or not they are still working. If they are, keep plugging along. But if they aren't, or you see an opportunity to do a little tweaking, it's time to switch things up.

Writer's Block May Be Saying Our Writing Isn't as Good as We Think It Is

Maybe, just maybe, writer's block is trying to tell you something about your writing. Maybe it's too bland or too predictable. Maybe you're focusing on statistics too much instead of telling a story. My writer buddies constantly tease me when I say aloud things like, "I don't know. This story I'm writing isn't speaking to me yet." I know it sounds silly. But what I'm trying to say (mostly to myself) is that it just doesn't work for me. Something is missing. And if it doesn't work for me, then it's not going to work for anyone who reads it. When these situations come up, I find it easier to suck it up and start over again in a way that will work. This may mean reviewing my notes and finding a different angle. It could also mean loosening up and thinking outside the box—perhaps going so far as to tell a story in a way that I wouldn't usually tell it.

When writers are blocked because their writing is coming out substandard or mediocre, it can help to think about things in a different way or from a different perspective. For example, while working on a blog post about how being emotionally happy often helps writers churn out their best stuff, I struggled to find the best way to explain what

I meant in a way that would make sense for the reader. A lot of time passed as I sat there waiting for inspiration to strike, and to be honest, it was extremely frustrating. I was trying to write that being mentally, physically, and emotionally happy often helps writers churn out their best stuff. I just couldn't come up with the best way to explain what I meant until I thought about my friend Maithen Elizabeth. And that's when it hit me—write about this from the perspective of an artist. Maithen is one of the best artists I know. She can take any idea, whether it came from a client or her imagination, and paint a custom piece that's guaranteed to make people smile. She had always told me that her secret sauce was to start by being happy. If she was in a bad mood, she wouldn't even think about picking up a brush. It was the same if she was stressed, sick, or tired. Being in a happy place was where all her best "stuff" came from, and writers—remember, we are artists in our own right, too—can be even better if we focus first on being happy.

Remembering Maithen's perspective took me outside of my zone and unlocked my block. Often, trying things a different way when your writing isn't working may do the same for you.

Writer's Block May Be Saying We're Working Too Much

As much as I love to write, too much of a good thing can be draining and lead to writer's block. We all need to know when to step away and take a mental breather. Go work out, play with your kids, spend time with your family who loves you, or hop on Facebook and "like" every post you see. Whatever floats your boat other than writing, do it. When you come back, that bout of writer's block will be a thing of the past.[8] Every writer I talk to says the same thing about "walking away" or taking a break from work and how beneficial it is. Even if they lie down in bed and watch their ceiling fan spin for thirty minutes, it's better than trying to force something to happen with their writing that simply isn't going to happen. When I took a break to help my son color his rainbow fish, it diverted my attention away from work just long enough to reset and spark my creativity. There are a variety of options. Lately, I've been making a habit of playing a *Madden* football game on my son's PlayStation 4 in the middle of the day as a tension breaker. There have been times when I'm so wrought with writer's block or stressed from working too much that I just say, "Forget it! I'm taking a nap to reset." On other days, I may go for a walk around the block or on a nice long run. I hate to admit this, but I'll even watch senseless videos on TikTok if it means giving my mind a break. Find whatever works for you.

Writer's Block May Be Saying It's Not Time to Write

Writing when you're not prepared to write is a futile endeavor. If you're angry, tired, not in the mood, not feeling it, or if it's not the right time of the day for your brain to be working, then wait! I'll be sitting on the couch watching TV with my wife, and she'll say, "You said you have to write some stuff later tonight, but all you're doing is sitting around. Why don't you just start now?"

My response is always the same: "Because it's not time to write." Sometimes, you have to know when it's time to write. Writer's block taught me a long time ago that if I just listen to my body and my brain, I'll know when it's time to write.

Writer's Block May Be Saying We've Lost Our Confidence

We always talk about the negatives of writer's block, but I heard somewhere that good writing is never quick or easy. Writers must maintain a high level of confidence, optimism, and even a sense of humor. Every time I struggle with and ultimately overcome writer's block, I build a little bit more confidence in my writing. My thought process sounds like, "I beat it once, I can do it again."[9] This is a real mental technique that leaders and business coaches always reference. Regardless of what you do for a living, you must have enough belief in yourself that you will find a way to overcome your self-doubt.

When you begin to struggle with self-doubts that eat away at your confidence as a writer, take some time to do the following:

1. Remember why you want to be a writer.
2. Take pride in what you've accomplished.
3. Ask someone to read what you've written and brainstorm other ideas.

We all want to imagine writer's block as this big bad meany akin to Thanos wielding the Infinity Gauntlet. But sometimes, it's closer to a health condition like exhaustion or illness that we can work to cure. We need to examine the various reasons why writer's block might have such a tight grip on us. We have more control over writer's block than we think. Getting through it is easier said than done, but it is possible.

Twenty-Five Ways to Stay Inspired as a Writer

When you love what you do, inspiration is not hard to find. It's all around us. Here are twenty-five additional ways to get out of that creative rut and stay inspired:

- Change the time of day you write
- Take breaks
- Change scenery (coffee shop, home office, park)
- Keep a journal of ideas
- Read books/articles from favorite writers
- Join a writing community
- Mentor a young writer
- Reward yourself
- Get organized
- Smile more (writing is fun, right?)
- Break larger goals into smaller pieces
- Write about something different
- Gain more experience
- Listen to music
- Don't beat yourself up
- Don't take yourself too seriously
- Have fun with/talk to your kids, friends, family
- Eliminate distractions
- Exercise
- Use a calendar and set time limits for projects

- Remind yourself of your goals
- Track your progress
- Read motivational writing quotes and funny memes
- Interview other writers about what inspires them
- Write your own list of what inspires you[10]

How to Beat Writer's Block on a Deadline

Despite all the useful messages writer's block may send us, there are situations where you may simply have no time to deal with it. You're writing on a deadline. You need to think on your feet, write with purpose—and do it as fast as possible.

Any writer who says they've never busted deadline is lying through their teeth. It may be by thirty seconds or fifteen minutes, but they've done it. We all have—countless times. You just don't want it to happen all the time or bring it on yourself. And when busting deadline is unavoidable, you want to mitigate the damage by taking as much control over the situation as possible. Here is a story to help set the stage for what I'm talking about.

First came the email at 10:31 p.m.

"Hey, Steve . . . you about done with your game story?"

Then, I saw my cellphone light up with a text. Three more minutes had passed. "Not sure if you got our email. We need your story now. Wrap it up, please?"

Luckily, I had just finished attaching my story to a reply email and pushed send before the background light on my phone screen faded to black. I breathed a sigh of relief and looked around to realize that I was the only one still left in the parking lot. All the stadium lights were off; every car around me had driven off.

"Dang it, Steve," I said to myself. "Busted deadline again."

I was furious with myself. At the same time, I felt like I had done everything I could. The high school baseball game that I was covering that night went into extra innings, and the last out wasn't until 9:58 p.m. That meant I had thirty-two minutes to grab a few quick quotes from a player or coach and somehow rattle off a five-hundred-word recap by 10:30 p.m. I mean, who would blame me for busting deadline given the circumstances, right? Five hundred words is a lot for that amount of time. Unfortunately, that's no excuse. Though there are extenuating circumstances from time to time, all writers—especially journalists—are expected to meet their deadlines. It's a requirement. If you bust once every blue moon by a few minutes, that's one thing. You may not even catch any grief at all from the copy desk or your superiors. If it's something that happens all the time and you're not doing anything to fix it, it could be a fireable offense. At a minimum, you won't be trusted in the clutch.

I've made deadline more times than not. But in this particular instance, I got back to my truck at 10:13, pulled up a Word doc, and got ready to type. But the thoughts weren't flowing. Writer's block! At the worst possible time! I had just watched eleven innings of playoff baseball and had plenty of fodder to pique a reader's interest. And still, I literally had no idea how to start this game story. I was sweating bullets as I typed up a few options for my lead paragraph. All of it sounded like garbage! I hammered that delete button. After seven minutes, I was still stuck on the first sentence. My mind was racing a mile a minute. Then, it hit me. Finally! Inspiration! I started typing, moving frantically from one sentence to the next. I pulled something workable together and shipped it off. There wasn't a single factual or grammatical error, and I busted by only four minutes. Still, I didn't make any friends on the copy desk that night.

I've operated in a deadline-driven world as a writer for a long time, and it's certainly not for the faint of heart. On some nights, I've had as much as an hour to write a story. On others, I've had twenty minutes or even ten. There have also been situations where I've been asked to have a brief recap ready to send as soon as the game ended. You just never know what you'll be hit with from game night to game night. There could be delayed starts, lightning delays, injuries, extra innings, or overtime. The list goes on. But you have to roll with it and be prepared for anything. It's the life of a journalist. Still, even when I was just starting out, it was never the deadline that bothered me. It was always that freak-out moment when writer's block sat on my chest like a five-hundred-pound sumo wrestler—ten minutes before I was supposed to file my story.

As I said earlier, we often bring writer's block on ourselves. And that includes situations where we are on deadline and expected to churn out our best stuff. The question is how we are to outwit writer's block when we're racing to beat a deadline, and there's little time to process our thoughts. Fortunately, there are a couple of workable fixes.

I think it's important to say that while many of the examples and tips in this section sound like they are talking to journalists (and they are), there will be a time in every writer's career where they don't have time to deal with writer's block. After all, most writers lead a deadline-driven life, whether they're journalists who have to submit an article or successful authors trying to get a book written in time.

So if you're a young writer sitting in an introduction to writing course and you have no idea yet if you're even interested in journalism, that's totally okay. You're going to face a deadline sooner or later! And when you do, many of these strategies can be adapted to your scenario.

When you're on a deadline and you just don't have time for writer's block:

Write as things are unfolding. The night I busted my deadline by four minutes, I didn't open a Word doc until I got back to my car. That's right—I hadn't even started writing anything about the game yet. This might have been a forgivable offense if I'd had more time to write, but I should have been thinking ahead to the possibility of extra innings or some other calamity. Any veteran writer covering current events makes every attempt to write as things are unfolding or new information is presented because, well, whatever can go wrong and bog down the process usually does. And you need to be able to react. This is a valuable lesson for so many young writers because so much can go wrong. And when you're young, you don't always know how to react. I now think about a potential lead throughout the night. I jot down key plays or situations between innings or during breaks in the action. Most of the time, I'll even craft a too-soon-to-print story shell in my notebook or on my computer. This way, even if the game takes too long or momentum shifts in the other team's favor, I've at least got something written down. This tactic helps me be as efficient as possible on deadline. It also helps to avoid writer's block because I'm not starting from scratch in crunch time.

Know your deadline and communicate. Sometimes, there's a difference between a deadline and a hard deadline. A deadline is when whoever you are writing for would prefer to have it. A hard deadline is when they absolutely must have it to go to press on time. For example, my deadline may be 10:30 p.m., but depending on the circumstances, I may be able to push it to 10:45 or 10:50 if a game goes past deadline or literally finishes with no realistic shot of me hitting the initial deadline. If I see that a game is taking longer than normal, I always communicate with the copy desk to let them know. And at that point, I'll ask what my drop-dead deadline is and if I'll need to write shorter. It's simply the right thing to do so that everyone knows what to expect.

Do your homework. Homework isn't just for students. When I know I'm about to cover a big game, I sit down beforehand and compile as much key information as possible so that I do not have to search for it later. This could be something as simple as each team's record coming into the night to key stats, history between the teams, and anything else that will give me some background. In some situations, I'll take that information and write a winner's story and a loser's version for the team I'm covering. I'm completely making stuff up when I do this, but believe it or not, many times, the game has played out exactly how I've written it in my shell—minus the actual stats and final score.

Look for inspiration in your surroundings. There have been countless times when I've gone down onto the field after a game with no clue how I'm going to write a game story with a quality opening. So I start looking for pieces of inspiration—however small or big. Sometimes I listen to what the coach says to his team after the win or loss. Maybe I take hold of a passing remark from a player during the interview. Maybe the vibe from the crowd or how they reacted is particularly noteworthy. My inspiration can come from anywhere. More often than not, using this tactic helps me create a foundation to springboard off of when I sit down to write. I may be getting a bit too deep when I say this, but I believe as writers, we should always be paying attention to our surroundings. And by that, I mean things like the weather, how fast or slow someone speaks when they are explaining something to us, the expressions people make when they walk into a room or are placed in an uncomfortable position. Practice paying attention to even the most minuscule of details, and then try to describe them with the written word. For example, I noticed once that a person that I was interviewing always leaned back in his chair and put both his arms behind his head every time he started to reminisce. It was a neat little quirk that most people wouldn't even notice or point out, but I did. I appreciated the subtlety of it, and it gave my writing more depth as I shared the story. I've also made a habit of keeping track of all the funny quips, sayings, and situations that have popped up over the years between my wife and kids. Mostly, I share them to Facebook. But someday, I could see myself creating a book out of those funny sayings. And occasionally, they provide the right inspiration for my writing. You never know when something completely unrelated will spark creativity in a pinch.

Keep it simple. To avoid writer's block and hit that deadline more often than not, focus on writing tight and with shorter sentences. Get to the point quickly and focus on the who, what, when, where, and why. Here's an example:

> All Aaron Judge has done lately is hit home runs. The Yankees' star outfielder blasted his fifth home run in as many games Tuesday, this time a 3-run shot in the bottom of the 11th inning to lift New York to a 4-2 win over the Mariners.
>
> New York tied the game at one in the bottom of the ninth inning, but Seattle took the lead and had the Bronx Bombers down to their final out when Judge stepped to the plate.

I literally just made this up and wrote it in two minutes as an example. This is what creates the backbone of a story, and if it were a real story, I should be able to write the rest of it very easily. Make a point to add some personality and storytelling to whatever you're writing, but don't get too fixated on anecdotes that take too long to develop. You can save those for follow-up stories.

Stay focused during your interviews. When you interview for a story, know what you want to ask your source and stick to that. For example, if a game ends on a walk-off home run and you have limited time to ask questions, stick to things like, "What went through your mind as you watched the ball go out of the park?" or "Take me through that at-bat. What did you see?"

If you know that was the player's first homer of the year, you could ask, "That's a great time to get your first home run. Tell me what's going through your mind right now."

There are so many other questions you can ask, but if you're on a tight deadline and only have a minute or two, you'd be better off sticking to the most important information that readers will want you to share with them. If not, you'll get stuck in a rambling interview that chews up precious time. Sometimes, I'll say, "Sorry, I only have a quick minute to get this filed, but I've got to ask . . ." Lead the conversation, get what you need, and start writing.

Get all the information you need. Besides getting hit with writer's block, there is no worse feeling than sitting down to write something in a pinch and finding out that you are missing one or two important details. Maybe you forgot to ask the right questions, or you failed to grab an important detail. You may be in a rush, but don't make things worse by missing any critical steps. This will throw you into a mental tailspin and make writing your article that much harder. As a journalist, you should observe events for an upcoming story and write down everything you're going to need as if you're creating a to-do list. Once you think you have everything, and before you leave to go write, ask yourself, "Do I really have everything I need?"

Don't delete. A lot of thoughts ran through my mind as I was writing this book. Some of them were good and others not so much. But I didn't delete any of them until I knew I was ready to turn in a finished product. I simply pushed them to the side for safe keeping. The same goes for when you're on deadline for work, school, or anything else and need to write quickly. You may write down different things as you try to find the right words. It's a lot of trial and error, but keep everything until you've finished the story. You never know when you may need to breathe new life into a piece.

A deadline can mean so many things. A feature writer could be given a month or a couple of days to turn a piece around for publication. Contributors writing stories for a local newspaper may have deadlines a bit further out. Students rely on teacher syllabi for their deadlines. Whatever its format, a deadline is a deadline, and there are real-life consequences if a writer doesn't hit it, from not being trusted to take on larger and more important assignments to losing clients or your job.

Try these strategies if you find yourself writing on deadline:

Read the directions. The easiest way to meet your deadlines is to know everything about the type of writing assignment you've been given. Look at the topic, the required word count, the details that need to be included (citing of sources, research, etc.), and how long you have to finish. Understanding what is expected will go a long way in helping you avoid writer's block *and* meet your deadline.

Communicate. Whether you're writing for a class or an organization has given you the opportunity to write something for them, it's important to understand their expectations. And like I said earlier, communicate sooner rather than later if you think hitting that deadline is going to be difficult.

Create an action plan. Determine the steps you need to put in place to make this assignment happen. Who do you need to talk to, and by when? How much research do you realistically need to do? If it's a longer piece and you need to break it into smaller chunks, how many words can you realistically write each day to get it done on time?

Don't procrastinate. If you are given a deadline that's a week or so out, don't fall into the trap of resting on your laurels. Deadlines come and go fast, even for novelists who could have a year to plan for a big project. The time to start planning, researching, and writing is now—especially while everything is fresh on your mind. I've always found that the second I started to procrastinate, I got hit with several other assignments—all with different deadlines. Then, I'd fall into this scheduling nightmare where I'd have to figure out what needs to get done now, what I can squeeze in later, and what can wait just a little longer while still not busting any deadlines. It's a lot to manage, and then you start writing too fast for your own good to compensate—which leads to writer's block and a potentially horrible or rushed finished product. I stopped procrastinating a long, long time ago, and it was the best thing I ever did.

You may not deal with a lot of deadlines right now, but I guarantee that you will eventually. It's the nature of the writer life. So start finding what works for you. Writing faster without feeling like you're putting much effort into it is a skill that all writers should master.

To summarize, remember that writer's block happens to everyone at one time or another. It doesn't matter if you're an aspiring writer or someone who has been published hundreds of times over the years. But the idea that we don't have control over writer's block, even if we are faced with a pressing deadline, is simply not true. Rather than point the finger at writer's block, take a look at what you're doing—or not doing—and how that may be contributing to the problem. Slow down, eliminate distractions, and improve your time management so that you have more time to write. Get all the information you need ahead of time, know your deadline and communicate, and write as things are unfolding. If you do all of these things and seek out other solutions that work best for your specific situation, you'll find that writer's block is more controllable than you think.

Writing to a Purpose

6

The Wide, Wonderful World of Writing

"You gotta keep trying to find your niche and trying to fit into whatever slot that's left for you or to make one of your own."

—Dolly Parton

I think it's cool when someone says, "I'm a writer." Why? Because no two writers are the same! Writing is also one of those professions where the options to utilize your talents are practically unlimited. This is especially true nowadays.

So when someone says, "I'm a writer," my response is always:

"Great! What type of writer are you?"

The answers run the gamut, and that's fascinating to me. The writer next to you could be an accomplished novelist with a dozen best sellers, or they could be a writer with more than forty years of experience who has never written a book before. They could be a sportswriter, speechwriter, or could be like me and enjoy writing all sorts of content.

Even novelists can go in fifty million directions—there are many different genres of fiction.

What type of writer are you? If you're getting started as a writer or have a few years under your belt but want to reinvent yourself or try something new for fun, here are just a few creative options to explore:

Novelist	Journalist	Creative Writer
Screenwriter	Lyricist	Content/Copywriter
SEO Writer	Grant Writer	Speechwriter
Blogger	Satirist	Short Story Writer
Poet	Playwright	Scriptwriter
Technical Writer	Marketing/Ad Writer	Legal Writer
Ghostwriter	Social Media Writer	Columnist
Travel Writer	Food Critic	Movie Critic

Finding Your Niche: Specialization

There are plenty of writers who specialize in one area and are perfectly content with sticking with it for their entire careers. There are a few reasons for this.

1. They have the most experience in this area.
2. Their comfort level is extremely high.
3. They enjoy writing about one particular topic.

I have buddies who have been sportswriters for their entire careers. Even though they could easily branch out and write about other topics, you won't catch them writing an advertorial or a feature on a local mom-and-pop business. They just don't want to—and that's okay. Meanwhile,

I know other journalists who write about city council meetings, but they won't be caught dead writing about sports or blogging about the latest in teen fashion. I also have a client who pounds out two or three fiction books a year. This is all she does.

If you can put yourself in a position where you can write about what you really know and enjoy, then you've hit the jackpot as a writer. Your writing will have depth and perspective, you'll be creative, and if you do it long enough, you'll become the authority in that area. As a result, there's no telling what doors will open up for you.

Take my buddy, Ben Baby, for example. If memory serves, when I first met him, he had just gone from being a night clerk at the *Denton Record-Chronicle* to covering high school sports full time. Not long after taking the job, he made the career-defining decision to take a post doing the same work for a newspaper in San Antonio. He ended up covering a huge story in 2015 where a couple of high school football players from John Jay High School physically assaulted a referee in the middle of a game. The referee, who was watching a play unfold, was leveled from behind by one of the players as retaliation for something that was said or happened earlier in the game. Another player hit him after he had fallen. Allegedly, a coach told his players to "take out" the referee, and the entire incident was captured on video. Ben was there to cover what quickly became national news.

Ben made an even bigger name for himself. More importantly, he was a consummate professional the entire time, and it showed how much he knew the topic and his craft in his writing. Ben ultimately ended up working for the *Dallas Morning News* covering college football and then hit an even bigger break when he began covering the Cincinnati Bengals in 2019.

From the day I met him, I have always been extremely impressed with Ben's work. No matter what he wrote, I was going to read it. I still do. And he's a perfect example of what can happen when you write what you really know and enjoy.

Finding Your Niche: The Chameleon

Some of the best professional writers are the men and women who write about that one thing they enjoy, but there's something to be said for the writing chameleon. This is someone whose niche is being versatile enough to tackle any industry, any topic, and any type of writing. Do they have their favorites? Sure. For example, I *love* writing about sports and have spent most of my career doing just that. But like a baseball player who can hit from both sides of the plate, if I need to write something on poverty, crime, or on the latest medical advancements to treat concussions, I can adapt and write compelling content as if I'd been writing about it forever.

If you can become a pro at seeking out the story, constructing narratives that audiences enjoy, writing clearly and understandably, and consistently finding the human-interest element to draw everyone in, you instantly become extremely valuable to a lot of organizations. I've said this in some of the blogs I've written, and I'll repeat it: what has made me a more effective writer is my passion for writing about any topic. It has improved my range as a writer, and I believe it has made me a more valuable partner for organizations that always need quality writers. This includes:

- Newspapers
- Magazines
- Small businesses
- Public relations firms
- Marketing and advertising agencies

I've written for newspapers such as the *Denton Record-Chronicle* and *Dallas Morning News*, magazines like those published by Murray Media Group, and various advertising and marketing companies. I've also written for business owners ranging from financial services to chiropractors, medical companies, architects, and everything in between. It's important to me that people see me as a multifaceted writer, and over the years, it has brought me all sorts of projects.

A perfect example is a client of mine who owns a family law practice and has been my client for roughly six years. When we first met, I had just finished interviewing him for an advertising spread he had paid for in a local magazine. I was the freelance writer for that organization and had spent a great deal of time getting to know him for what turned out to be a twelve-hundred-something word article.

And he loved it—so much that he reached out not too long after to see if I'd be interested in ghostwriting blogs for his firm. He knew blogs were a great way to connect with existing and potential clients while also driving more traffic to his website, but he didn't have the time to write them himself. Naturally, I said yes. Fast forward a bit, and I've written a blog post for him every week for nearly six years! In between that, he's tasked me to write website content and bios for his paralegals and office staff. I even helped ghostwrite a book. I know him, his firm, and his employees like the back of my hand and can write content as if it came straight from his mouth. It's that ability to organically combine my words with his voice that has helped his law firm grow and keep this writing partnership going for as long as it has.

He also referred me to his wife, whom I helped write content for as she was growing her fitness company. And not too long ago, he referred me to another client who is a plastic surgeon.

There are plenty of writers who are just like me who don't mind writing about different things. I have a client who is a full-time nurse, but she loves being a storyteller and has written novels that range from sci-fi to action-packed thrillers, murder mysteries, and even sports. Recently, she banged out a romantic comedy novel. I respect her for being flexible with what she writes and being unafraid to put her stories out there for a variety of audiences—all of which have different expectations.

Choose the Writing Path That Works for You

Coming out of college, I imagined myself being a sportswriter for the rest of my life. I was a jock growing up, and I lived for enough free time to watch *SportsCenter* on loop for hours on end. Even all these years later, if you ask me what's my favorite thing to write about, I'll say sports every time. But as more time went on, I realized that as much as I love sports writing, I wanted to experience more of what the writing life had to offer.

I like the idea of being a chameleon—being able to write about family law or architecture just as proficiently as I can about touchdowns and home runs. And by opening myself up to that challenge, I was able to settle in, build confidence, and overcome many of the fears that previously held me back. So what type of writer are you? Perhaps you've been dreaming for years about being a novelist. Maybe you want to write for the *New York Times*. Possibly, being a skit writer for *Saturday Night Live* sounds pretty cool to you. Or maybe you see yourself one day being a speechwriter for the president. Or you could decide you want to write about it all—like me!

Whatever the case, be the writer you want to be. If you can do that, you are well on your way, my friends.

Of course, every type of writer has their own tricks of the trade, their own set of rules or guidelines that help them succeed in their chosen niche. As writers, we are constantly improving our craft, and I truly believe that we never stop learning and expanding our skills. For example, journalists may need to pay more attention to interviewing and active listening, while more purposeful character creation may be especially important to the novelist. In this section, we're going to talk about improving in both of those areas. We're also going to discuss how to get started when you don't know where to begin, how to "show" and not "tell" your reader what is going on through well-intentioned word usage, how to be a better storyteller, and so much more. So buckle up, ladies and gents—when you've found your niche, whatever it might be, you can really start writing with purpose.

7

How Active Listening Can Make You a Better Journalist

"When people talk, listen completely.
Most people never listen."

—Ernest Hemingway

In an article for *Poynter* titled "The Power of Listening," Chip Scanlan refers to a passage David Ritz wrote in *The Writer* that reads, in part, "Patient listening, deep-down listening, listening with the heart as well as the head, listening in a way that lets the person know you care, that you want to hear what she has to say, that you're enjoying the sound of her voice." The lines are evocative and paint a romantic picture of journalism. Writers who choose to be journalists should be passionate about the stories they tell. And to tell them appropriately, they must learn the art of active listening.

Active listening is incredibly important for journalists. This is true whether you are covering a game, learning every critical detail from a late-night smash and grab, interviewing a presidential candidate, or sitting in a classroom as your journalism professor goes over the differences between libel and slander. To be a good interviewer and ask the right questions, you must listen. To truly hear someone's story or the message they are trying to teach you—and get it right—you need to listen. To get people to talk enthusiastically, you have to shut up and listen. But not just any listening will do.

Years ago, I was mentoring a young journalist who, without fail, insisted on sitting down with me before a big interview to go over the list of questions he had prepared. He was so focused on not missing anything, to the point where (if I remember correctly) he had as many as twenty predetermined questions scribbled in chicken scratch on his little reporter's notepad. He hadn't even met with the person yet, so everything he had written down was anticipatory type stuff. But it made him feel prepared, which I thought was admirable. At least he cared, right?

So we went back and forth and fine-tuned a few things, and I was pretty confident by the end of the powwow that he had everything he needed. Thankfully, he felt confident too. But even though I had helped put his mind at ease, I made sure to tell him before he left that his list of questions—and his ability to talk—wasn't going to help him hear the interviewee or uncover the real story if he wasn't actively listening.

Active listening plays an important role in all areas of your life. It's a soft skill that not only improves communication between yourself and others but helps you build and maintain relationships, retain information in the workplace or at school, problem-solve, follow directions, be an effective leader, and more. To actively listen as a writer means fully concentrating on what someone is saying rather than just passively hearing the message of the speaker. It involves listening with all senses, smiling, making good eye contact, having good posture, and engaging in the conversation. It's a skill some of us have to work at, and it requires a lot of patience. The patience part is critical because it's easy to overlook the listening part when you're just starting as a writer. But when you get it down pat, it's like a whole new world opens up.

I'm not the only one who feels this way. The best journalists, writers, and storytellers are the ones who realize that active listening has a direct impact on your ability to craft a quality piece. Active listening goes hand in hand with interviewing and storytelling in that it will help you:

- Avoid relying on a long list of predetermined questions.
- Uncover and recognize the details people want to read about.
- Create natural back-and-forth dialogue.
- Get the best answers to your questions.
- Ask additional questions based on the speaker's response.
- Avoid misunderstandings.
- Build better relationships.
- Become a more effective writer.

There are several ways you can improve as an active listener, with benefits that will translate to your writing and to any source interviews you may conduct as a journalist or a researcher.

I didn't come out of the womb knowing all the ins and outs of being an active listener and how to conduct a solid interview. It took a lot of time and effort to cultivate the skill, and I fell on my face more times than I can remember. What helped me boils down to nine actionable steps. While these skills and tips may be most applicable to conducting an interview, they're useful to anyone observing or writing about an event. Active listening is useful to journalists whether they are writing a story based upon an interview or a story based on any live occurrence.

Show up on time. By "on time," I mean at least ten to fifteen minutes before the interview is supposed to start. This shows you are a professional who cares about the story, your craft, and the valuable time the other person is dedicating to you. It also allows you to walk in without feeling rushed and helps calm your nerves. When you eliminate some of this ancillary stuff that can take you off your game, your mind and heart will be open to listening.

Be clear about what you are there to discuss. When you begin an interview, you may know what you are there to ask or talk about, but that doesn't mean the interviewee does. Simply stating, for example, "I'm here to talk to you about the latest award your company won," or, "I heard a rumor that your starting quarterback injured himself in practice," helps to convey and clarify the purpose of the interview. Doing this sets the stage and enables you to guide the conversation *even though* you should be prepared to go in a different direction based on how the interviewee responds.

Listen when you don't know why you're there. As a journalist, you will encounter situations where you will speak to someone and have no clue what the nature of the conversation might be. Maybe your interviewee called you and requested the interview. Maybe a client wants to brainstorm a new blog topic that you haven't discussed yet. In these situations, it's best to allow your interviewee to guide the first part of the conversation. Listen intently the entire time, and then ask questions that help you understand what they are saying.

Be personable and engaging. Nobody likes a dead fish, and they're not going to open up to one in an interview setting. I always start with a smile (what a novel concept) and create small talk to break the ice and build rapport.[1] It's important to me that the person I'm speaking to feels like they can talk to me. I'll ask them about their day, their family, or something light that I had heard was going on—just to get the conversation going. If they tell me they've never done an interview before or are struggling to say what they really want to say, I encourage them and make sure they know they can take their time and that I'm here to help. You are there for them; don't ever make someone feel rushed.

Focus on learning something new. When you talk to people as a journalist, keep in mind that you don't know everything. If you did, you wouldn't be talking to this person. Look at them as someone who can teach you something and go so far as to ask them to tell you something that you probably would never know. I start my questioning with basic questions—even if I know the answers. This gets the person you are talking to in teaching mode. It also gives them the respect that they deserve. In all my interactions with people, whether it be personally or professionally, I've always taken an interest in learning something new.

Ask stupid questions and clarify. When you write articles based upon interviews, you have to be able to explain the simplest of details to your readers. So don't be afraid to ask what you think are stupid questions so that everything makes sense to you. After all, dumb questions don't always lead to obvious answers. Furthermore, if something is confusing—or even if it's not—ask for clarification. If the interviewee is talking about things you don't understand, ask them to explain. This is also critical in making sure you heard them right. Say, "So that I heard you correctly, did you mean . . . ?" This is a safeguard to make sure you don't write misinformation later. Don't allow the interview to end until all your questions are answered.

Don't multitask. As you run interviews, don't be thinking about the next two or three questions you want to ask while the person is talking. You may not end up asking your preplanned questions in order. Focus on listening to what your interviewee is saying in the moment, and then ask follow-up questions that matter. You'll usually find that your initial questions organically pop up during the conversation. If it helps, using a recorder is better than trying to frantically write down every word someone says. It also allows you to focus more on having a conversation.

Ask open-ended questions. When the person you are interviewing is a Chatty Cathy, life is great. But that's not always the case. Open-ended questions require more than a one-word answer, and they help get you the information you need to tell the story. A couple of good examples of open-ended questions are, "How did you know your plan would work?" and, "Why do you think everyone responded the way they did?"[2]

Don't forget the details. When you conduct interviews, some of your early questions may be broad, and that's fine. But once you've got a good conversation going, get more granular by asking specific or more pointed questions, such as, "How does this work?" or, "What made you think this would be the result?" Questions like these really get someone talking. They may even apologize for giving you too much information! Never agree with them when they do. Tell them that it's always best to have more information than not enough. There may be an important detail buried in that excess information, and now you have it!

I've worked hard on incorporating these nine steps into every conversation I have as a writer, regardless of whether I'm meeting someone for the first time or I've known them for years, and it's allowed me to tell some pretty neat stories. A perfect example is a lady named Alicia. Full disclosure here: Alicia and I had been friends for years, and I already knew she was a former softball player at Tarleton State University in Stephenville. I also knew she still played in a few recreational leagues. But what made her story interesting was that she was an accomplished Mary Kay independent beauty consultant full time. So basically, by day, she was all dolled up selling makeup and skincare products and making women feel and look beautiful. By night, she was wearing eyeblack, spitting sunflower seeds, and diving for hard groundballs in a softball game. And she did all of this while being a loving wife and mother of two young girls.

Her story was screaming to be told, and so I wrote a feature on her for the local newspaper. But just because I knew some of the answers to my questions didn't mean I knew the whole story. So I started from ground zero, starting with what I already knew and giving her a chance to fill in the details. The back-and-forth conversation led to plenty of revelations that really made her story pop. For example, I had no idea that her parents, Norm and Debora, rarely missed a college game and made it a point to track down every ball Alicia hit over the fence—all thirty-one of them. I learned how she once played in Europe and tried out for Team USA, and I was able to recount how devastated she was when she didn't make the cut. I spoke to her parents, her husband, her former coach at Tarleton, and even her director at Mary Kay. And what came from all of those interviews, listening, and back-and-forth dialogue was quality storytelling with depth, emotion, and energy. The article was exactly what I hoped it would be going in. But it was my ability to strike a balance between asking the right questions and actively listening that took it from a basic story on a mom who juggles a career with softball to a feature that gave the reader a real peek behind the curtain to this woman's life. I had so much information and detail that I remember feeling like I could have written a book on her.

I believe that focusing on active listening, drawing inspiration from the world around me, and making sure I get the most out of each interview allows me to write in ways others can't. And I believe it can do the same for you. Sadly, I've seen plenty of situations where writers completely miss the boat on riveting story angles because they don't actively listen. The young reporter I mentored with his list of questions had made this mistake in the past. It had been his habit to prepare what he thought was a fail-safe list of questions only to sit there frozen like a deer in headlights two minutes in when the person he was interviewing went in a completely different direction than what he was anticipating. His list of questions became worthless! He would get so busy trying to write everything down that he stopped listening and fumbled through a few questions that didn't have any bearing on anything.

He had seen his interviews end way faster than he anticipated. He left feeling like he hadn't heard the full story or asked the right questions, and he had written stories he knew didn't live up to what they could have been. So he would try to prepare even more for his next interview. But his problem wasn't his preparedness—it was that he wasn't actively listening and adapting when the real story presented itself!

Stuff like that happens all the time to writers. I've come a long way, but I can remember one instance very early on in my career when I went into an interview after having covered a game and, I kid you not, literally asked the coach a question that he had already spent five minutes answering to a crowd of reporters—including me. Where the heck was I? I can tell you where . . . I was buried inside my reporter notepad, looking at my own list of questions. I wasn't listening, and it showed. The coach's team had just lost, so he was already on edge. It didn't shock me when he said, "Steve, I literally just gave you my answer. Wake up!"

When you're reporting or interviewing sources for research purposes, do yourself and your interviewees a favor: focus on being the best active listener. If you do, I promise you that not only will the more appropriate questions organically spring to mind during the conversation, but you will come away being able to tell a much better story. In some cases, you may uncover a completely different story than you thought you had going in. You'll end up a better reporter than you were—and a better writer.

A Few More Tips for Journalists

There's so much that goes into being a respected and prepared journalist who takes pride in their job. Here are a few tips you might not have thought of:

- **Know your beat.** A beat is specialized reporting, like sports writing, education writing, or crime writing, that you do every single day. Regardless of what beat you plan on covering, the goal is to know it inside and out. By doing so, you set yourself up to provide insight and commentary that no one else would know.

- **Be fair.** Never sacrifice your integrity, career, or the career of someone else simply to get the story first. Odds are that sometime in your career, you will end up covering a sensitive topic, and your sources must feel like they can trust you and that you will be not only accurate in your reporting but fair.

- **Stay hungry.** Make yourself available and be willing to cover anything, from a football game to a local fair to a city council meeting. Not only will it make you a better writer, but your bosses will think of you before they offer a story to anyone else.[3]

8

Research and Organization: The Hallmarks of Good Nonfiction

"I didn't set out to write this book. It crept up on me when
I wasn't looking, when I didn't know I was writing it."

—Mark David Gerson, *The Voice of the Muse*

For years, my mom begged me to write a book. Not just any book, though—a children's book. She felt it would bring out my sensitive side. She pointed to how effortless it was for me to write about my kids on social media and in shorter blog posts. If I could do that, why not do something longer—and for all kids? It was and still is a really sweet idea but not something I could put my whole heart behind. I wanted to write a book eventually, but I just didn't see myself starting with fiction. I felt more comfortable with a nonfiction book. Nonfiction is based on real people, real events, real places, real topics, and real problems. Nothing is made up or fantasized like in fiction, so your goal as the author is to explain or inform about a concept or situation that you are uniquely qualified to discuss and do it in a way that is entertaining, educational, thought provoking, and spurs people to see your point of view.

I loved the idea of nonfiction so much better—simply a personal preference. As for the topic I'd choose? Well, that would eventually come to me when the time was right. I wasn't in any rush. So I waited many years . . . and politely told my mother no every time she brought up the children's book idea.

Then, one day, it hit me. I was going to write a book for writers. After all, I have over twenty years of experience and unbridled passion invested into what I do for a living, plus a slew of tips, tricks, and thoughts—some original, and others passed down—that I was sure would be valuable to all types of writers. Had other books for writers been written before? Of course. A few really good ones that spring to mind are *On Writing Well*, *The Elements of Style*, and *The Poets & Writers Complete Guide to Being a Writer*. And there are many more where those came from. But by the same token, the same can be said for books on weight loss, leadership, religion, politics, or health and wellness. And avid readers are quick to snatch up the titles that resonate with them the most. So why not write about what I *really* know, and then add my point of view?

I was enthused! I was ready to do it! Then I wondered, "Wait . . . how do I write a nonfiction book?"

You're likely reading this chapter because you've asked yourself the same question. Maybe you're a beginning writer who has tinkered with the idea of writing a nonfiction book and finally wants to make the jump to being a published author. Perhaps you're midway through your first book and need help getting to the finish line. You could also be a fiction writer who wants to try your hand at nonfiction. Maybe you've built up a portfolio full of poetry, blog writing, journalism pieces, short story creative writing, and magazine feature writing and now want a few organized thoughts on long-form writing. Maybe you're just a glutton for punishment! Just kidding! Writing a book of any kind is an incredibly worthwhile endeavor and a major life accomplishment.

On paper, writing a nonfiction book seems easy enough—just sit down and start writing. But we all know if it were that easy, everyone would be an author. That's just not the case. Plenty of people say, "I have a book in my head that is waiting to be written," and nearly all of them want to pull the trigger. Very few of them do, though. I don't know how accurate this statistic still is, but as recently as 2019, several online sources stated that 97 percent of people who start a book don't finish it. In my opinion, it's not because of procrastination, trying to be too perfect, or even writer's block—although those are legit obstacles. It's largely because they don't know how to turn an idea with so many moving parts into reality. They don't know where to start, what to do next once they have, or how to finish. They may even underestimate how long it can take. The good news is that writing a nonfiction book that you can be proud of is possible. If you take a deep breath, put the necessary legwork in, and find a real problem you can solve for your readers, you will be ahead of the game. My goal with this chapter is to provide a few tips and tricks that, God willing, help get you there faster.

If you want to write a nonfiction book, but you're not sure how, follow these steps:

Pick a topic you feel strongly about. To write anything of value in nonfiction, you have to *know* the topic you're writing about and *feel strongly* about it. Otherwise, why have you committed to writing a book in the first place? For most writers, this is the easy part. Just pick a topic that resonates with you personally. If you have many topics that interest you, start with the one that makes the most sense. For me, it was writing.

For you, it might be mental health, weight loss, estate planning, or how to live your life pain-free. If you feel passionate about what your book is about, then your writing will reflect that.

Tim Stevenson wrote a book called *Better: The Fundamentals of Leadership.* After serving as a successful leader with four organizations, Mr. Stevenson became a Master Sherpa Executive Coach and founded Stevenson Leadership Coaching. He had also written eight books prior to this one, so clearly, he'd established himself as an authority on leadership. At the end of a section on body language, manners, personal presentation, and how leaders are constantly being read by those around them, Mr. Stevenson wrote the following:

> There's an old story passed down for more than 200 years. A Virginia man was standing by a riverbank trying to figure out how to get across. Along came several men on horses, who proceeded to ride across the stream. The man watched the first and second riders go by, then he asked the third man for a ride. The third man agreed, and the Virginian rode across the river behind his host. Afterward, an excited person confronted him: 'Do you know who that was? That was Thomas Jefferson! Why on earth did you ask him for a ride?' The man replied, 'I didn't know it was Thomas Jefferson. The first two men had faces that said, 'No.' I asked Jefferson for a ride because he had a 'Yes' face.' There are people whose faces say, 'Welcome.' There are others whose faces say, 'Beware of the dog!' Are you aware of what your face says? What do you want it to say?[1]

Tim doesn't get too broad here. His topic is leadership, and he manages to stay in that lane throughout what is ultimately a 238-page book.

I love this passage because it goes to show how there is so much more to leadership than having an important title and a handful of people under you. It's how you carry yourself, your body language, how people perceive you, and the message you are portraying—whether spoken or unspoken. It takes a special person to be a leader. Rather than list off qualities of great leadership in a way that is bland or even surgical, Stevenson packages them in genuine, down-to-earth stories that have a better chance of resonating with readers. His writing is simple and straightforward, and that approach is relevant to all nonfiction writers. Furthermore, his anecdote is relevant to his point, and his passion for his topic shines through. Regardless of what your topic is, choose one that you're informed about, have experience with, and can share in a way that is relatable to your audience.

Determine your target audience. One of the biggest mistakes an author can make is not defining his or her audience. In other words, determining who they're writing for or talking to. Who are *you* trying to reach and educate, and what do you want them to take away from reading your book? Many times, we get so caught up in the excitement of writing a book that we forget who we are talking to. And when that happens, what we're left with is a finished product that underwhelms when it's finally on bookshelves or Kindles everywhere. Knowing who your audience is will help you determine:

1. How to go about writing a book that they need.
2. How to speak to them and their challenges, pain points, or interests.
3. The tone of your book (technical, easy reading, etc.).
4. What is already out there in the marketplace (books, blogs, research on your topic).

5. How you will structure your book.
6. Who you are going to market the book to after it is published.

This is something you want to have figured out well before you start the writing process. You don't want to make your audience too broad, you don't want to end up talking down to them, and you also don't want it to be so narrow that you pull the rug out from underneath yourself before you're published. When you are clear on who you are writing to and who would be interested in not only buying your book but actually reading it cover to cover and recommending it to others, it's a lot easier to write in a way that speaks to them. This book is a perfect example. My goal from the beginning was to have a book that is useful to all kinds of writers: first-time writers, veteran writers, nonfiction writers, fiction writers, freelance writers, college writers, high school writers, writers who own their own business, and so forth. And because of that, my pie-in-the-sky dream was to see it reach intro to writing courses in high schools and colleges across the nation. It wasn't that far-fetched of a goal, so long as I kept my audience in mind. Being a writer myself, it was easier for me to determine what my audience's pain points and interests were, and it was easier for me to keep it in my head that this book needed to cover everything. But early on, I found myself falling into a trap of only talking to a select few—journalists and bloggers. I had to take a step back, remember that I needed to stay true to serving all writers, and keep my target audience in mind from start to finish. As you work on your nonfiction project, you need to do the same. Of course, once you know your target audience, you need a plan for how best to talk to them.

Create an outline. One of the ways writers get hung up and don't ever start or complete their book is that they don't have a plan. They don't know where to start. If they do know where to start, and they get a few pages in, they don't know what they're going to do about the middle of the book. And even if they get there, they don't know how to put a pretty bow on the project. An outline is one of the best ways to remedy these issues. It's a hierarchical structure for how you envision your book being laid out. With all stories or arguments, there should be a beginning, a middle, and an end, and everything you write should flow from one thing to the next. When you write your book's outline, ask yourself how you think your book should flow. Then, write everything down. It doesn't have to be perfect. No one else has to see it except you. And it could also change after you start writing, since the direction you are trying to go will become clearer as you go along. But by at least formulating some thoughts at the beginning and getting them written down, you will have a roadmap that serves your book's purpose and helps keep you on track.

Set a deadline. All projects need a deadline, so set one for your book. This also will help keep you on task. Start by looking at how long you anticipate this book will take to write and pick a date. Factor in your current work schedule and other responsibilities, how fast you type, how long you think it will take to gather supporting research, and how many words and chapters you expect to write. Everything that could impact your timelines. One tip for setting a deadline that is passed around often is to take the number of words you expect to write (example: seventy-five thousand words) and divide that number up into a per-day goal. This will give you a better indication of what your deadline should be. Maybe your initial goal is to finish by the end of the year. Maybe it's six months, or two years. It's completely up to you, but the goal is to honor whatever deadline you set.

Do lots of research and take plenty of notes. Doing research is pivotal to writing any book. So much has been written about every possible topic that you can't expect to sell a reader on your experiences alone. You must validate and confirm your experiences and arguments by reading other published work, referencing and citing other sources, and infusing arguments for and against your stance. Not to mention, you want to make sure what you're writing is accurate. This makes your book credible and authoritative. Your readers will trust what you're saying because you took the time to go beyond your own writing to see what else is out there and use that research as teachable moments in your book. It may also help you to look into what else is out there in your specialty area to see how those books are performing on the market. If a particular topic isn't doing well, consider going in a different direction entirely or approach the same topic from an angle that will resonate with readers. If you do, you will have a book that answers many of the questions the other ones didn't answer. It will be a leaner, meaner, and more comprehensive book.

Try not to do anything out of order. I don't know how other book writers will feel about this one, but I have always been a process-oriented individual. You don't put the cart before the horse. You have to learn to walk before you can run. In football, you have to catch the ball before you can turn and run with it. Even Stephen Covey wrote in his best seller *The Seven Habits of Highly Effective People* that Habit #3 is "Put First Things First" and Habit #5 is "Seek First To Understand, Then To Be Understood." There are just certain things you have to do first before you can move on to the next thing in life. And the same applies to the actual writing piece of your nonfiction book. Start with figuring out what you're going to write about, then come up with a working book title, organize your table of contents, write your acknowledgments and introduction, and then get to writing each chapter one after the other.

Following this step-by-step format (in that order) helps keep you on track as you move through creating a legit manuscript. Will you likely need to circle back and change things as you go? Absolutely. Is there a possibility that you will have to go back and add chapters after you think you're done? Yes. This absolutely happened to me with this book. But by doing things in order as much as humanly possible, you are organically carrying momentum from one task into the next one—thereby creating flow and natural transitions in your writing and helping you track your progress. Writers who start their book by doing things out of order, including writing chapters out of order (chapter 10 before chapter 6, 3 before 1, etc.), run the risk of having inconsistencies or lack of continuity and cohesiveness from one chapter to the next that they'll end up having to fix later. On top of that, readers might be put off if your book reads like it skips around.

With that being said, I'm not completely against the idea of "skipping around." I wrote a lot earlier in this book on writer's block, and writing out of sequence has been known to be an out-of-the-box tool to help overcome those moments where you just can't find the right words to keep going. For example, if you can't figure out how in the world to write chapter 9, but you already know how you're going to end the book, you can skip straight to the end while your creative juices are flowing. I can see how this would be a much more powerful tool for fiction writers than nonfiction, but if you experiment with it in nonfiction and find that it helps get you where you want to be with your book, then I say run with it.

Tell stories. Actually, tell lots of them. In any long-form writing, readers will expect stories. As humans, we remember them better than any rigid concept or rule you could possibly throw into a book—especially when they contribute to the purpose of the book or whatever it is you are trying to write. Here is a good example of storytelling and how incorporating these elements into your writing not only hooks a reader and makes them want to read more but also resonates with them on a personal level.

> There's a photo on my wall of a woman I've never met, its left corner torn and patched together with tape. She looks straight into the camera and smiles, hands on hips, dress suit neatly pressed, lips painted deep red. It's the late 1940s and she hasn't yet reached the age of thirty. Her light brown skin is smooth, her eyes still young and playful, oblivious to the tumor growing inside her—a tumor that would leave her five children motherless and change the future of medicine. Beneath the photo, a caption says her name is "Henrietta Lacks, Helen Lane or Helen Larson." No one knows who took that picture, but it's appeared hundreds of times in magazines and science textbooks, on blogs and laboratory walls. She's usually identified as Helen Lane, but often she has no name at all. She's simply called HeLa, the code name given to the world's first immortal human cells—her cells, cut from her cervix just months before she died. Her real name is Henrietta Lacks.[2]

This passage is from the very beginning of the book, *The Immortal Life of Henrietta Lacks* by Rebecca Skloot. See how the author chooses her words carefully and with almost surgical precision as she takes what could be a mundane topic on science and medicine and puts a human face on it? This subject she is describing is more than just a code name in a medical journal. She's a real person. Storytelling is the number-one way to get your point across, make what you're trying to write easier, and keep readers engaged at the same time. And you can tell lots of stories without sacrificing your goal of being clear and concise.

Ask for feedback. One thing I made a point of doing before I reached out to a publisher was to give my book to a few colleagues and friends to see what they thought. I was confident that they'd like it. But were there any glaring omissions? Did any chapter not make sense? Were there any irrelevant passages? What should I expand on? What should stay and what should go? Could they see themselves reading it cover to cover without being forced to? Who wasn't I speaking to yet? I didn't go into any of it with the expectation that I would take all of their advice. At the end of the day, it's my book and my voice. And honestly, there is plenty of bad advice out there. But I kept my heart and mind open because I wanted this book to be the best it could possibly be. If it made sense, I was completely open to adopting those ideas. By asking for feedback, I could gain insight into what I couldn't see in my own writing. I could bounce ideas off of them and get differing points of view. All of it helped me fine-tune this book to create a final version that has a smooth, logical, and powerful flow with all the necessary transitions.

Understand that you're in this for the long haul. Where many wannabe authors trip themselves up is thinking that writing a book is easy or that it can be accomplished in a few weeks. Maybe that could happen for you. But for the vast majority, it's hard. It feels like a monumental project—because it is! To start a nonfiction book—and then see it through to completion and publication—takes a commitment to being invested for the long haul, no matter what obstacles come your way. There's lots of research, rewrites, positive and negative feedback, line edit after line edit, and times when you simply need to start all over again. There are times of self-doubt, writer's block, and busy schedules. Also, what you thought was a rock-solid chapter order ends up getting moved around or added to. What do you do then? Do you throw your hands up and quit, or do you roll with the punches? The key to writing a book is to go in knowing that it will be one of the more difficult projects you've ever tried to complete. Embrace it. Take it chapter by chapter, and you'll get it done.

The final chapter of this book takes a deeper dive into getting your hard work out there for the masses to enjoy. But it's worth saying now that at the end of the day, a book really isn't a book unless you actually get it published. Once you figure out how to write a nonfiction book, make sure you share it. It doesn't do anyone any bit of good to have a beautiful manuscript collecting dust on a closet shelf.

Let's keep the spotlight shining on the book writers of the world and use the next chapter to dive into writing fiction novels.

9

Writing Fiction People Will Want to Read

"The difference between fiction and reality?
Fiction has to make sense."

—Tom Clancy

In 2018, my father-in-law, Dennis Ault, finally published a book he'd been sitting on for the better part of twenty years called *The Adventures of Pete the Fire Engine*. Pete was a 1930s era Peter Pirsch fire engine, a style you commonly find in small-town stations. While he always did good work and was a fan favorite for kids all over town, Pete was also getting old. When a new fire engine with all the bells and whistles shows up in town one day and quickly earns everyone's favor, it's clear Pete's days in the town of Adams Mills are numbered. As sad a direction as this book was headed, the good news is that there is always a happy ending in children's literature. Dennis didn't disappoint in his delivery. I won't ruin the ending (it's worth the read), but the moral to the story was that although circumstances in our lives may change, we can still be valuable and make a difference.

My family immediately fawned over the book, as did I. It was a short story—roughly twenty-two pages total. It had simple sentences, an easy-to-follow story arc, and a wholesome message. Bravo! Here I was thinking I was the only writer in the family, and then Dennis, a retired firefighter and EMT with a heart of gold, cobbles together this children's piece seemingly out of nowhere.

"Just don't tell my mom," I thought to myself.

Needless to say, Dennis was the first person I called when I sat down to write this chapter. I wanted to know how the process went for him. Specifically, how long it took, his process for writing the book and keeping tabs on all his ideas, any pitfalls he ran into, and the most difficult part of the experience. Not a lot to ask, right?

Dennis's answer, however, was the complete opposite of what I anticipated. Essentially, he admitted that he wrote his book in about an hour and a half—all while waiting for his truck to be fixed. The idea for the book literally hit him while he was seated in the waiting area. He previously had no plans to write a book. He had no characters or storyboard. There weren't any long nights of staring up at spinning fan blades in his bedroom, hoping to come up with an entertaining concept. His book literally popped into his head and said, "Write me." And naturally, as if he had already read chapter 4 of this book, he had a pen and notepad handy. He handwrote what came to his heart. He lived by what I've been saying in this book, which is: write like you mean it. And the result was a book for every child to enjoy. I know our family will certainly treasure it forever. I thought it was amazing how quickly he wrote the book and that he finally pulled the trigger and had it published after all those years.

Young writers might be thinking, "It must be because it's fiction, right?" After all, fiction is completely different from nonfiction. It's make-believe. It's people, places, and events that are imaginary. And there are so many directions you can go that it can feel like the world of fiction is your oyster. With a blank canvas to work with, perhaps fiction writing is . . . dare I say . . . easy?

Wrong! There is a tremendous amount of freedom that comes with creating your own world and story, but there is so much that goes into it—things like characters, character development, story, plot, subplots, plot twists, dialogue, a worthy climax, setting the scene, showing instead of telling—that it's impossible to expect every novel to fly onto the page with ease like Dennis's children's book did. Your story, whether it's about an old fire engine or a tale of best friends who find themselves trying to outrun a serial killer in the forest, must hook the reader and make them want to read it from cover to cover. And that usually takes quite a bit of time. Many aspiring authors get hung up on not having enough time to do everything above. It's too complicated. It's scary too. "Will anyone actually read this besides my mother?" they wonder. "What if a publisher won't pick it up?" I get it; breaking into this world as an author isn't easy. But clearly, people like Dennis do it all time.

So how do you become the next great fiction writer? How do you write your next book like you mean it?

Write what you love and know. What made writing about Pete the fire engine easy for Dennis was that he is a retired firefighter. He knows that world. It was his life for a very long time, and he loves it. Being a fireman is in his blood, and I imagine there is a lot of Dennis in Pete. Dennis was once the young guy at the station, and as the years went by and he got a little older and wiser, he continually found ways to prove his value despite being surrounded by a bunch of younger guys. So it's no wonder his book was written the way that it was.

Granted, you don't have to be a firefighter to write a book about a fire truck. The same goes for writing a fiction story about alien abduction if you've never been abducted, witches if you've never been possessed, or ghosts if you've never seen one. Don't feel like you have to limit yourself. Have fun. See where your imagination takes you. All I'm saying is that most first-time novelists gravitate to something that helps them hit their stride faster. As J. K. Rowling said, "Write what you know: your own interests, feelings, beliefs, friends, family, and even pets will be your raw materials when you start writing." Even if a wannabe novelist tries to write something outside their comfort zone, there is usually something embedded into the story that resonates with them and puts their personal stamp on the project. As I write this, I'm reminded of a client of mine. She's a nurse who writes novels and novellas on the side and has me edit them. While the topic for each novel runs the gamut (sci-fi, sports, romance, thriller, murder mystery), they all have at least a couple of medical scenes, such as paramedics arriving to a crash scene and conversations between doctors who are hurriedly trying to save a girl's life. It's a writing device that helps her craft some of her best stuff, and I think that's a great approach.

Read, read, read. There are so many novelists out there whose words are beautiful and stories so captivating that it's difficult to put any of their books down for even a millisecond. I mentioned J. K. Rowling. This chapter opens with a quote from Tom Clancy. There's also Stephen King, F. Scott Fitzgerald, Jane Austen . . . the list goes on and on. As a young writer (actually, all writers), whether you want to write fiction, nonfiction, or magazine articles, you must also be a devoted reader if you expect to hone your craft. More importantly—and this is something I mentioned earlier—read with a critical eye. What did you like or dislike about what you read? What worked and what didn't? How would you have written it differently? Read published work from anyone and everyone—classics, trash . . . it doesn't matter. You will learn something from all of them, including what makes a good book. You may try to emulate them at first, and that's okay. Eventually, you'll find your own style and voice.

Create an outline. Creating an outline in fiction writing is just as important as creating an outline for a nonfiction piece. With all stories—even the made-up ones—there should be a beginning, middle, and an end, and everything you write should flow from one thing to the next.

Create a character chart. When you're writing a novel, especially one with several characters—all of whom have different names, backstories, personality traits, descriptions, ages, motives, and arcs—it can be very easy to lose sight of who is who. Timelines or family trees can become confused. This not only makes the writing process more difficult but can lead to an unintended plot hole if you aren't careful. For example, imagine creating a character early on in your book. They are killed by a sniper bullet midway through but then randomly end up in a bar scene later in the novel with one of your other main characters. To avoid mistakes like this, before you start writing, create a character chart. At first, you may have only one or two characters on there and may think of it as a fruitless exercise. But it's so worth it. Take the time to immerse yourself in the world you've created and dive into who you want each of these characters to be.

- What are their full names, ages, occupations, family tree, and importance to the novel?
- What do they look like?
- Are they a villain? Are they a hero? Something in between?
- What is special about this character?
- What motivates them?
- What does their character arc look like?

You may not have all the answers to these questions right now, and that's okay. And maybe some of these examples won't matter as much with what you're writing. But if you slow down and invest enough time in this strategy, you'll be more organized, you'll understand each character better, there will be fewer inconsistencies in your writing, and you'll have a better novel overall.

Set a deadline. Having a hard deadline that you hold yourself to will keep you on task. As I said in chapter 8, take the number of words you expect to write (example: seventy-five thousand words) and divide that number up into a per-day goal. This will give you a better indication of what your deadline should be, and then it's up to you to honor whatever deadline you set.

Research. If you're wondering if you'll have to do any research with fiction, the answer is almost always yes. Doing your research is just as critical with fiction writing as it is with nonfiction. Why? Whether a writer is trying to pen a realistic mystery novel or an action adventure in space, they need to make sure that what they write makes sense where it needs to. For example, if a character has symptoms of PTSD, it's important the writer know what those are and how they manifest themselves. If you're writing a murder mystery, you may have to know how long bruising remains on a dead body. If your characters are traveling between cities and states, it might be a good idea to know how long it takes to make it to each location. Well-done research can be the difference between a classic novel and something that not only won't hold a reader's attention but also destroys your credibility. And who wants that?

When it comes to research, there are plenty of resources to consider:

1. Online. Isn't everything on the internet these days?
2. Videos, movies, documentaries. YouTube, a few movies on Netflix, or some other media source is bound to have something that will kickstart your research.
3. The library. This is old-school. But it's still highly effective, especially if you're writing about something historical or need to trace family histories, etc.
4. Existing novels on a similar subject matter. If you're writing a mystery novel, you may want to study books like *The Da Vinci Code* or *The Cuckoo's Calling*. If you're writing a horror book, pretty much read anything by Stephen King or even Mary Shelley's *Frankenstein*.
5. People you know or can get introduced to. Talk to an expert. If you don't know someone who is, see if any of your friends and family can connect you with someone who is. If that doesn't work, find someone online and either give them a call, send an email, or meet them for coffee or a Zoom call.
6. Field research. Sleep in your car for a night to know what it's like to be a character who is homeless. Go to the police station and see if they'll lock you up in a holding cell for a few hours. Okay, that one would be interesting. But it could work.

As you collect research, you have to keep tabs on it and stay organized.

For online research, I create a Word doc or spreadsheet with important links broken down per topic. I also bookmark each site I need to keep track of on my laptop. Take a page from what I wrote about organizing the writing process. Any notes or interview recordings can be transcribed on a basic Word doc and referred to later. Buy a few binders or folders and use those for larger documents that you need to keep track of (maps, printouts from the library, etc.). Also, back everything up! Remember, it's all fun and games until your laptop crashes or is destroyed somehow.

Have an enticing beginning. When you're writing fiction, you have to hook the reader and invite them into the story you've created. And just like any party you invite someone to, you want them to take their coat off and stay awhile. Some of the best fiction writers this world has ever known have said they spend the majority of their time on the first few sentences. And it's because those first few words will make or break everything that comes after it. Just like a terrible foundation will destroy the house that's built on it, a lackluster opening leads to a mediocre novel. Here are just a few examples of great openings. If you're an avid reader, I'm not sharing anything new here. But these lines are worth their weight in gold.

> It was the best of times, it was the worst of times, it was the age of wisdom, it was the age of foolishness, it was the epoch of belief, it was the epoch of incredulity, it was the season of Light, it was the season of Darkness, it was the spring of hope, it was the winter of despair.
>
> —Charles Dickens, *A Tale of Two Cities* (1859)

The sky above the port was the color of television, tuned to a dead channel.

—William Gibson, *Neuromancer* (1984)

Call me Ishmael.

—Herman Melville, *Moby Dick* (1851)

If you really want to hear about it, the first thing you'll probably want to know is where I was born, and what my lousy childhood was like, and how my parents were occupied and all before they had me, and all that David Copperfield kind of crap, but I don't feel like going into it, if you want to know the truth.

—J. D. Salinger, *The Catcher in the Rye* (1951)

Dickens introduces poetry to the beginning of his novel, as well as explaining that his world is a world of contradictions. William Gibson uses a vivid, unusual metaphor to both strike the reader with his creativity and set an undeniable mood. At the beginning of *Moby Dick*, Melville intrigues his readers by suggesting "Ishmael" might not be the narrator's actual name. And in *The Catcher in the Rye*, J. D. Salinger immediately takes control of his tone and establishes a commanding personality for his narrator. He also immediately declares he intends to defy traditional storytelling conventions.

All of these openings present a little something different. Some are quick and to the point, like Melville's three-word opening line. Others are longer. But they all get you wondering, "What's going to come next?" It makes you want to keep reading. What your beginning looks like, feels like, smells like, and tastes like is up to your imagination, and the idea is to get your readers to use theirs from the very first line. Create intrigue, startle your readers, catch them off guard with something they wouldn't expect to read. If you're writing a sci-fi piece, start in space with a battle between star destroyers. If a murder mystery is more your cup of tea, start with someone coming across a dead body hanging out the front window of a coffee shop. If it's a drama, set the mood. Make the reader want to turn to the next page, and then the next. If you do this, you'll find that the rest of the novel is easier to write.

Remember purpose. You're writing a book, so the natural thought is to just write, write, write, and write some more. But there has to be purpose to what you're writing, and it's important to be clear and concise with how you approach each sentence. Every character must contribute to the story or the reader's understanding of the world it takes place in. Every scene or conversation must serve the plot or character development. Anything beyond that is fluff and could probably stand to be deleted.

Show, don't tell. Do you want your readers to be passively involved in what you're writing, or do you want them pulled into the story? This is the difference between showing and telling in its most basic form. Telling a reader is more or less a basic statement of an action or emotion. Like, "Jack was cold." And by doing that, you keep the reader at arm's length when you should be allowing them to experience the action or emotions for themselves. You're telling the reader what they should see or feel instead of allowing them to feel it. Showing allows the reader to draw out their own conclusions, develop an image in their mind, be pulled into the action, and become invested in your story. Here are a few examples of showing versus telling.

Telling: Jack was cold.
Showing: Jack shivered uncontrollably in the ice-cold ocean.

Telling: She was angry.
Showing: Jane's eyes burned a hole through her adversary.

Telling: Steve walked down the street.
Showing: Steve walked a few hundred yards, stopped to smell the flowers a few times along the way, then casually opened the restaurant door to grab a bite to eat.

The idea of "show, don't tell" is easy to understand. It's much more difficult to apply. So don't get bent out of shape if you're not perfect at it the first time. Allow yourself room to grow and keep looking for ways to incorporate it into your writing style. Here are a few tips to help you implement this principle into your writing:

- Focus on dialogue, body language, and actions/reactions.
- Be specific in your descriptions.
- Use strong verbs (hammer, whirl, justify, yell, damage, purchase, undermine).

Read aloud. Writers should read their stuff aloud. Not only does it mentally help you catch things like grammar mistakes, inconsistencies, clunky sentence construction, missing words, and more, but for fiction writers, it's a great tool to more effectively establish characters, dialogue, improve rhythm and pace, and determine how each character should sound different from each other. Just like earlier in this book where I wrote about how using a pen and paper first can be good for writers, reading aloud is one of those strategies many take for granted until they give it a try and notice how much value it really does bring to their writing.

Finish. As I said before, the last chapter in this book will go into how to get your stuff out there and published. But I can't stress enough the importance of finishing. When I was talking to Dennis, he shared that he started his book on Pete back around 2001. Yes, he wrote it quickly. Yes, it only took him a few more hours to get it properly edited. He even had his sister do the illustrations. But then he sat on it. Five years went by, then ten more, and no story on Pete. He said *Pete* probably would have been collecting dust somewhere to this day if it weren't for a commercial he happened to see about a publishing company. At that point, he finally got working on finishing what he started all those years ago. And now he can call himself a published author! How cool is that?

Even if you follow all the tips above, it can still be difficult to recognize where your writing falls short. So once again, don't be bashful about asking for feedback. Inevitably, someone is going to catch something that doesn't make sense, doesn't add value, or could be spruced up with a more deliberate use of words. This is what you want because, after all, you want the finished product to be the best it can possibly be. So if an editor says, "Hey, this really needs a lot of work," don't just say okay and go back to the drawing board. Ask them for specifics, and have some back-and-forth dialogue. Not only will you unearth your best stuff, but it will also be exactly what your audience wants to read—and can't put down.

10

Storytelling: Not Just for Novelists

"Tell your story. Don't try and tell the stories that other people can tell. Any starting writer starts out with other people's voices. But as quickly as you can start telling the stories that only you can tell, because there will always be better writers than you and there will always be smarter writers than you, but you are the only you."

—Neil Gaiman

Writers don't just write. It's so much more than that! The act of writing should be a deeply personal relationship between authors and their words, and the finished product should consistently reward the reader with an opportunity to feel every moment of that process through raw, captivating, and intentional storytelling. At our core, we aren't just "writers." We are storytellers. And regardless of whether you're a journalist, blogger, or a nonfiction novelist, every writer should have that innate desire to go beyond the normal process of putting words on paper and tell a story people want to read.

In 2017, I was sitting in my office frantically trying to log on to my laptop to see how a recent feature story I wrote turned out. The story had been posted on the *Denton Record-Chronicle* website overnight, and I was eager to see what type of reaction it would get. After all, I had spent the better part of three or four weeks working on it—interviewing doctors, parents, athletes, etc. I had a vested interest in the project. After a quick glance to make sure everything looked good, I copied the article link and shared it to my social media accounts. I was confident that it was a great story, but how many people would actually engage with the posts and read the article? More importantly, would they like it?

That's the goal—for people to click and read what you write, right? Sure, the likes and retweets are great and all. But they pale in comparison to knowing that someone actually took the time to read something you wrote—and enjoyed it. This is especially true for longer pieces such as this one. Luckily, I didn't have to wait long to find out. Not only were people noticing the posts, but they were reading the article, commenting on it, and, in some cases, sending me texts and calling. The newspaper's social media was also blowing up with comments. The next day, I got a call from the doctor I had interviewed for the story. His phone lines had been blowing up with new patient requests.

The entire experience restored my faith that in an age of increased technology and a push toward disseminating content through video more than the written word, people still enjoy reading. This is especially true when the writer focuses on poignant storytelling that is relatable.

Can you imagine how I felt that night before, waiting for the chance to hear what people thought? Of course you can. As a writer, we all crave that validation—no matter if it's our first time being published or we've been there and done that a thousand times over. And as we wait, a riot of emotions consumes us—nervousness, anxiety, trepidation, excitement, cautious optimism, and everything in between. The waiting game is agony for me. It always has been, and perhaps more so for this particular piece. Yet I sign up for it over and over again because I love what I do. Just like you, I put my heart and soul into every word I type. It means something to me. That story, and the hundreds of others that came before and after it, had a piece of me in it—even if I wasn't the central character.

Deep down, though, I was confident everything would be okay. Because I believe that readers love a good story. Just as I did in the story above about having to wait for a positive response from readers, in the article itself, I put a face on the experience. I told a relatable narrative that helped readers connect with my writing, feel something for the person and family I was writing about, develop an understanding for the broader topic, and live out a genuinely happy ending. Here's part of the article:

> Jackson Weatherford stares at every baseball field as if it were his home — a home, sadly, he may never go back to.
>
> In May 2015, Weatherford, then a senior at Guyer High School, took a 90-mph fastball to the left side of his head during a playoff game. The blow was so powerful it sent his batting helmet flying as the ball rolled back toward the pitcher's mound. He turned 180 degrees and, with his back now to the mound, began to collapse.
>
> "I remember being in the [batter's] box and seeing the pitcher's leg come up," said Weatherford, who was caught by the home plate umpire. "The rest is fuzzy. It wasn't until the next day that I began piecing everything together. I asked my mom, 'So can you fill me in?'"[1]

This feature was a continuation of a long series of investigative articles we had written over the course of a few years on concussions and their impact on sports. It was an important series to write because when people think of concussions, they instantly think of the bone-jarring hits of football. But concussions can and have happened in any sport—baseball, volleyball, soccer, etc.—and the ramifications are life changing. It's a hot-button topic when you think about player safety, not just in-game but also for their long-term quality of life, which is why we continued to write about it.

When our editor, Scott Parks, charged us with this task, his goal wasn't just for us to write about stats and figures. That's boring. No . . . to get a topic like this to truly resonate with our readers, we knew we had to tell a story. We had to put a human face on each article. We had to get in the trenches and talk about a big-picture topic through the eyes of someone who has experienced it firsthand and was willing to talk about it—players, coaches, trainers, doctors, helmet manufacturers, professional athletes, and parents. We wanted to get granular and zoom in on how concussions continue to impact real people and what was being done about it.

The idea for this particular concussion story came to me when I heard about a man named Dr. Chad Stephens and the fantastic work he was doing with interventional concussion management and migraine treatment. He was using a minimally invasive device that was doing wonders for breaking the cycle of postconcussion symptoms. And naturally, I wanted to tell the world about it. But I also knew that readers wouldn't be near as engaged if I simply focused on a device or procedure. That's where Jackson came in. I didn't cover the game where he got beaned, but one of my colleagues did. When he brought up the fact that Jackson was still suffering from postconcussion symptoms, a gigantic *ding! ding! ding!* went off in my head. This was a kid who, when he attended his high school graduation, had to wear sunglasses and could only be in the room long enough to go on stage to accept his diploma. On top of that, no one in the auditorium could clap or even make a sound.

It was a horrifying story on so many levels, and it made me wonder, what if I could connect Jackson with Dr. Stephens?

Jackson's dad, Mike, was still an assistant coach at Guyer and had watched the injury unfold before his eyes. Imagine being in that position as a parent. Even as a coach on the field, with more access than any average parent in the stands, he was powerless. He told me that even weeks later, he slept on the floor outside of Jackson's bedroom door—just so that he could be there at the drop of a hat. I visited Mike and Jackson in person to see what they thought about me writing an article. It was a follow-up on Jackson and his life after the concussion, but it would also feed into the big-picture issue of concussions, share stories from other athletes, and introduce a doctor who apparently had a device that could break the cycle of postconcussion symptoms. Along with Jackson, I interviewed a young lady named Madison who suffered a concussion after being kicked in the face during a high school soccer game. It was the beginning of a wild journey that saw Madison recover from her injury only to fall ill and later be diagnosed with celiac disease. She developed headaches and, after more complications, began experiencing concussion-related symptoms. As she explained, it was almost as if the soccer injury had just happened. The cool part about Madison was that she had already visited with Dr. Stephens before my article. She had participated in his procedure and was recovering.

This particular article netted me an award from the Associated Press Sports Editors and received rave reviews from readers. More importantly, it gave me the chance to bring two people together who otherwise never would have met. Jackson tried Dr. Stephens's new procedure and saw positive results. Did it clear up everything right away? No. But there was suddenly a light at the end of the tunnel for a kid who tried to make the best of a life that had been turned inside out. I was also able to build a very close, trusting relationship with Jackson and his father. I still bump into them every now and again, and it's great to see that the harrowing experience in high school no longer defines Jackson.

Storytelling can take your writing beyond a connection to your audience and make an actual impact on their lives. This is that amazing moment when writing goes beyond words, mechanics, and research and becomes transcendent. As writers, we must write compelling content in a way that speaks to the reader. Whatever you write should be easy to read and make the reader want to keep reading. But more importantly, as you push the story forward, each sentence should evoke emotions such as anticipation, sadness, fear, relief, surprise, or anger. If your readers don't experience those emotions, maybe you should try harder with how you're telling stories. It has always bothered me when I read something with no passion or imagination. I call it the "white noise effect." Much like a snowy picture on your TV when it has little or no signal, if whatever you're writing is robotic and reads exactly like what everyone else is churning out, then you've accomplished nothing besides putting everyone to sleep.

Here's an example of what I'm talking about:

Okay opening: "Vivian Gray, a star player at Argyle High School, has signed to play college basketball at Fort Lewis College. Gray recently led Argyle to a state championship and had offers from the likes of Texas, Baylor, Rice, and Oklahoma State."

Better opening: "Argyle's Vivian Gray could have gone anywhere to play college basketball. She just redefined anywhere.

"Gray, one of the nation's most coveted high school basketball recruits, whose suitors include Texas, Baylor, Rice, Oklahoma State, and others, confirmed Tuesday she will sign this afternoon with Fort Lewis College — a Division II program in Durango, Colorado — on the first day of the early signing period."[2]

You can also go shorter, like this example I found in several places online. Edna Buchanan, a Pulitzer Prize-winning crime reporter, wrote a story about an ex-con who, on one drunken night, stumbled into a Church's Chicken. The man was told there was no fried chicken, only nuggets. He punched the woman at the counter and was eventually shot by a security guard. Buchanan's opening sentence: "Gary Robinson died hungry."

Whether you're a journalist, blogger, novelist, feature writer, or dabble in another form of content or copywriting, it is important to be a storyteller, connect with readers, and write in a way that gets them to turn the page.

Here are a few time-tested tips on how to be a great storyteller:

Put a human face on it. Anne Frank put a human face on the Holocaust. Rosa Parks put a human face on the civil rights movement. People want to read about people. It just makes what you're writing about more understandable and compelling. More than just reading stats and figures, they want to see how an important event, social issue, or topic affects an ordinary person or group of people. They want to go on a journey with these people and experience all the things they experienced. I believe this tip works for whatever you are trying to write about. Let's say you're a student, and you need to write something on racial injustice in the deeply fractured world of 2020 and how that compares to the civil rights movement in the 1960s. Rather than regurgitate a bunch of stats and refer to quotes from people you weren't even alive at the time to talk to, wouldn't it be more captivating if you wrote the paper through the eyes of someone you can talk to? A person. A business. An entire family. What are they experiencing? What's their backstory? How are they uniquely involved? What's their message?

Be an active listener. I wrote about this tip in more depth in another chapter, but it is important to throw in here as well. The best storytellers are the ones who realize that active listening makes you a more effective writer. Rather than waiting for their turn to speak, they listen for clarity and understanding before responding. This not only eliminates misunderstandings but shows respect to the person you are speaking to. Whether you're reporting or researching for another kind of writing, if you're too focused on what the next question is on your notepad or you aren't opening your eyes and ears to the bigger story, you won't be listening and will likely miss out on the real depth or meat behind the story and the person who is sharing it with you.

Focus on a great opener. Once you've found the face of your article or whatever you're writing, take your time and set the stage. A great opening tells a story but also hooks the reader with crucial information and makes an otherwise mundane article stand out. I'd go so far as to say that in the reader's eye, a great opening separates a good writer from a great one. With that said, writing a quality opening isn't easy. I've found that writing the first two, three, or even four paragraphs of a detailed piece to be incredibly time consuming and draining from a creative standpoint. But once the foundation is set, and I've got it where I want it, the rest of the story flows so much easier.[3]

Don't be robotic. No two stories are the same, so stand out by thinking outside the box. Ask yourself, what is the story about, and how would the reader want this presented? How would I want this story presented to me? I tell my clients all the time that the last thing you want is for the words on your website to be uninviting, stilted, robotic, and just like everyone else's. If you own a dentist office, what story can you tell about your company and the services you offer that will help you stand out from all the other dentists of the world? That's what should make up the bulk of your website copy. The same goes for car dealerships, law offices, banks, plumbers, and everyone else. Each professional website should give its business a clear and authentic voice! I once wrote website copy for a community bank. They pulled me in after they had paid someone else to write their copy, and they wanted me to fix it because the copy sounded too much like something you'd find on a big-bank site. It didn't represent them at all. So I stepped in, and thankfully, the end result was something they could be proud of.

Focus on unique storytelling. Similar to not being robotic, resist the temptation to follow down the same path someone else went. In other words, you never want a reader to be thinking, "I've heard this story before." Be creative. Get personal. Throw in a few unique twists. Ask the right questions, so you can tell the story in a way no one else has.

Make it understandable to the reader. Scott Parks once told me (and I'm paraphrasing), "Your readers shouldn't have to work hard to understand what you are trying to tell them. They should be able to cut through each sentence of your story like a hot knife going through butter." Understandable writing involves an understanding of the mechanics of writing and writing in the active voice. There should be a beginning, middle, and end to your story. Sentences should be clear, concise, and easy to read. You should explain as much as you can, going so far as to answer any question a reader could ask.

Build relationships. I build rapport and trust with everyone that I come into contact with. And not necessarily because I'm a writer but because I just really like people. I love getting to know people, making new friends, building trust, interviewing them in person versus over the phone, and finding out what makes them tick. When you have that growing circle around you, the stories that people really want you to tell fall into your lap. You're now the perfect writer to tell that story. You can be creative and provide insight and details that no one else would know.

Read other storytellers. I mentioned this before. You can learn a lot from what other writers do, regardless of whether they knocked it out of the park or swung and missed. I promise you that the true storytellers are easy to spot. Implement what you learn into your writing.

Try this: Scour the internet, a newspaper, a magazine, or even rows of books at your local bookstore. Find something you wouldn't normally read or be interested in, and then read it. Did the author make it interesting? How? What was it specifically that made the piece worth reading? What did you like or dislike? Did they speak to you or at you? What resonated with you the most?

I shared the early manuscript of this book with a friend of mine named Mike. Now, Mike is this big, burly pest-control guy. And while he appreciates quality writing and is a grammar fanatic like the rest of us, you won't catch him reading stuff like this book. And that's the reason I wanted him to read it! I wanted to see if something he wouldn't normally pick up in a bookstore would hold his attention. At least from what he told me, it did! I made it interesting for him, and that gave me even more confidence as I pushed to get this book published.

Work for it. Keep practicing your writing. And just when you think you've practiced enough, practice some more. Read your stories out loud to other people and see what type of reaction you get. If their reaction doesn't exceed your expectations or leaves them asking questions you didn't anticipate, go back to the drawing board. If you read your work and it doesn't even make sense to you, it's time to rethink your approach. And that's okay, by the way. The first draft is never perfect.

Great storytelling transcends all types of written work, and if you do it correctly, your writing will go from mediocre to compelling. With that said, great storytelling takes time, so invest the time to become better at it. It's much easier to pencil whip an article, blog, or book just to get something out there. But will anyone read it? Will anyone relate to it? Is that tactic worth your time? Will it make you a better writer? I say no.

The human brain is hardwired to respond better to storytelling. It's why mom and dad always read us a good book at bedtime, and it is why we stand around the proverbial water cooler at work. We can't wait to hear or read what happens next.

So don't just write. Be a storyteller.

Four Reasons Why Being an Extrovert Can Make You a Better Writer

While introverted writers are flat-out amazing at what they do, I'm also a firm believer that successful writers can be somewhere in between or be full-blown, happy-go-lucky extroverts. In fact, there are quite a few perks to being an extroverted writer:

- **Extroverts pull inspiration from anywhere and anyone.** I can't tell you how many times I've found great story ideas while having a conversation with someone at a networking mixer, charity event, or even my son's baseball games. Extroverted writers are great at character development and utilizing authentic dialogue. We're highly descriptive, and all of that translates to our writing and being able to tell a story.

- **Extroverts write about anything.** Even if an extroverted writer isn't a pro at understanding legal jargon or writing about the latest real estate trend, they are willing to learn it. They will seek out the right people and put themselves in situations they aren't used to.

- **Extroverts grow their client lists organically.** What professional writer out there couldn't stand for a few more clients? Networking and being visible in the community are at the heart of what I do. It's where I can tell my story, meet people, and hear their stories. A bigger client list means more opportunities to write. Extroverts are conversational by nature, so they're easy to talk to. Potential clients have a chance to get to know you while having that warm and fuzzy feeling that they are truly being listened to.

- **Extroverts educate other writers.** What better way is there to improve your writing and be a more engaged member of the world around you than by helping educate other writers? Everyone has to start somewhere. Extroverted writers want to do speaking engagements. They want to share their knowledge, and even their shortcomings. They are more inclined to educate students or take younger writers under their wing. That mentoring process makes the people you are educating better writers and makes you a better writer, too.[5]

11

Becoming a Successful Freelance Writer

"Why fit in when you were born to stand out?"

—Dr. Seuss

I am not the type of guy who takes risks. In fact, I'm always quick to joke that if I'm going to make any sort of leap in life, there'd better be a net to break my fall. And even then, I may think about it a few hundred times before committing. But I took a massive leap of faith in 2014 when I quit my job at the bank to get back to pursuing my passion for writing full time.

Between 2003 and 2014, I worked full time as a teller, followed by positions as a personal banker, assistant manager, and eventually branch manager. During that time, I continued to write as a side hustle, mostly for Allen Publishing. The owner knew my wife and happened to be looking for freelance writers, so I quickly jumped on the opportunity. In the meantime, I continued to juggle my born-again writer life with my banker life. But as entrenched as I was getting in the banking world, it just wasn't my thing. I loved the people I was working with and respected them immensely. I enjoyed being part of a team and having ownership of something. I also thoroughly enjoyed working with my customers; I developed a lot of really neat relationships with people in those days and felt like I contributed to making my community better beyond the walls of the bank. I took a lot of pride in it. At the same time, it wasn't my passion. My passion was writing. I believe in the adage that if you are doing what you are truly meant to do, then you'll never work a day in your life—and I wanted that for myself. Consequently, I kept looking for a way out of the banking world for many years. And when that didn't present itself organically, I finally decided that it was time to make it happen. That's right, I quit! I was scared out of my mind, and I hated the idea of letting anyone down by leaving. But I had to make the move for myself. And the awkward conversation with my wife went something like this:

"Honey, I'm quitting the bank tomorrow."

"The heck you will!"

Thankfully, I talked her into it and followed through with my plan. More importantly, I asked her to trust me. Look, I knew the whole idea reeked of failure. I was giving up a decent salary to chase a dream that historically doesn't pay well and isn't as stable as banking, selling insurance, or the medical field. But I also believed wholeheartedly that we should all do what we are passionate about. Sometimes, it takes drastic measures to make that happen. And I wasn't going to allow myself to fail.

So despite being as scared as I had ever been in my life, I took the proverbial plunge and from scratch created Edit This. While I would continue to freelance for several newspapers and magazines, the idea was that I could primarily work with small-business owners to handle their content writing needs—whether that meant writing blogs, website copy, newsletters, press releases, or advertisement copy. It was a novel concept, in my opinion. After all, I had worked alongside business owners for years as a banker, and I saw firsthand how much they had to juggle to make everything work. Whether it was keeping their employees and clients happy, paying bills, staying up to date on all the latest technology, focusing on growth, or even ordering supplies, these business owners had a lot going on. Sometimes, it was too much to get done in a single day. The last thing they had the time or the energy to do was find the right words for a blog post or wrap their brains around how to give their marketing strategy some pizzazz. I knew most business owners didn't have the time to write for themselves, didn't want to write for themselves (they hated writing), or couldn't write for themselves (they admitted they weren't good writers and needed someone to hold their hand). That's where I would come in as their "writer for hire." I used my words and creativity along with their voices to create content from scratch or spruce up what they had written.

I'd seen a need in the field, and I was prepared to fill it. I just didn't know where to begin or how to make myself stand out. After all, I'm not the only writer to choose from. Sure, there is a lot of work out there to be had, but if the list of quality writers who are competing against you for those opportunities is twice as long, how can you possibly stand out? All I had at the time was my computer, an enthusiastic attitude, and tons of creative juices. But I had only one client, and truth be told, that client was from an existing relationship with a newspaper. So really, I was starting from scratch as a freelance writer and small-business owner. If I wanted to stand out, I had to look beyond good writing skills, put myself out there, and say, "Hey, look at me!"[1]

Maybe you're in the same position—trying to sell your writing on an article-by-article basis as a journalist, blogger, or some other freelance writer. Regardless of what type of writer you are or what you specialize in, the goal is to help yourself and your writing stand out and be noticed first. Your client could be a business owner or a local magazine. They could be a book publisher or a major public relations agency. In any case, you want them to think of you first.

Networking and Building Relationships

It was my former life as a banker that helped me realize how important networking is for business owners. I remember sitting in a one-on-one with the president of the bank very early in my career and listening to him tell me all the reasons why he hoped I would be a better fit for that particular branch than my predecessor. He threw a lot at me, but the one takeaway I had was when he said that the branch had been there for almost ten years and no one knew. So in the course of my work for him, I put networking, relationships, and community involvement at the forefront of everything I did. And that was perfect for me, since I am a people person by nature. I showed up to every chamber meeting, every ribbon cutting, every mixer and luncheon, and as many charity events as I could. I joined several networking groups. I became a board member for the local chamber, and eventually its president. Was I a pro at it right off the bat? No. But in a very short period of time, I got to know everyone. They knew me, and when push came to shove, they knew my door was always open. Some of my best friends today are the strangers I met back then. When I left the bank to get back into writing full time, I had built a solid reputation as an active community member and an overall really nice guy. My circle of influence was bigger than I ever imagined, so even though I was taking a massive gamble by quitting, I never felt like I was doing it alone.

I don't know, maybe there was a net under me, after all?

When I told everyone that I was leaving the banking world for good, they instantly supported me. They loved that I was chasing my dreams. They saw value in what I was doing and wanted to know how they could help. I knew web designers, marketing gurus, graphic design artists, and even other writers who wanted to develop a synergistic relationship with Edit This. I was a one-person show, yet I had business owners in neighboring fields willing to work with me and introduce me to people they knew. It was a powerful feeling to know that I had developed that level of trust with people. And it still is. Today, I'm still an active member of the local chamber of commerce. I still have my favorite networking groups, and there isn't a mixer I haven't been to. And here's the kicker: that bank I was working at—they are now one of my best clients! They reached out to me a year or so after I had left to see if I'd help them with a few projects. At first, it was just small stuff like advertising articles in local magazines. Then it was their website, press releases, and a few blogs. They loved my writing style, but more importantly, they knew I could tell their story with the written word better than anyone because I was a former employee. I truly cherish the relationship I have with them now, and I will never forget everything they taught me.

Building authentic relationships is one of the best ways to grow a successful small business—especially for freelance writers. If people feel like they know you, they see you a lot, and they like you, they'll never forget you. They'll think of you when they have something that needs to be written, and they'll share their story with you.[2]

Do Good Work

Don't just write to write. Go above and beyond. Tell someone's story in a way no one has before. Help a small business connect with its audience in ways the owner never thought of. Help a local magazine connect with its readers by creating content that matters to them. When someone comes up with an out-of-the-box idea, don't dismiss it because it doesn't fit with your style of writing. See how you can marry their ideas with your own to come up with something magical. Bottom line: be passionate about what you do and let that show through your writing. When I sit down to write anything—even if it's a simple thirty-five-word employee bio for a website—I am putting everything I have into those thirty-five words and being as creative and unique as possible. And if not, then I'm not afraid to delete and start from scratch.

For an example, take a look at this before and after of a bio I did for a client who was looking to go beyond the traditional way of writing bios for his company. With a little direction and a few conversations, this is what we came up with:

Before: "Duaner Sánchez (born October 14, 1979) is a retired Dominican-American professional baseball player. . . . During his MLB career, Sánchez pitched for the Arizona Diamondbacks, Pittsburgh Pirates, Los Angeles Dodgers, New York Mets, and San Diego Padres. He is known for his distinctive sports goggles he wears while pitching."

After: "Duaner had an opportunity through Major League Baseball to pass his knowledge along to the next generation of big leaguers. He ultimately decided against that because he felt more passionate about working with kids—and he knew STRIKE was already ahead of the curve in that department. Duaner joined us in March 2020 and brings a wealth of experience from his playing days. By the time he retired in 2012, Sanchez had pitched for the Arizona Diamondbacks, Pittsburgh Pirates, Los Angeles Dodgers, New York Mets, and San Diego Padres. He was known for wearing sports goggles while he pitched, and he turned heads immediately by pitching 18 scoreless innings in his first 15 games. Not many people know this, but Duaner was originally signed as a shortstop. That gives him incredible versatility in terms of knowledge, which is something we want him to pass on to our kids. Duaner and his wife, Natalia, have been married for 14 years and have six kids between the ages of 6-18."[3]

It's not like my client's original bio on Duaner was bad. But when you're a small-business owner, you want to give potential clients every reason in the world to feel like they know, like, and trust who is working on the front lines with their child and that, as parents, they are getting real value for committing to this particular facility. If you notice, the nuts and bolts of the original piece were saved. But by interviewing Duaner and adding in that he has a passion for passing on his knowledge to young ballplayers, it shows his investment to the game of baseball. Not to mention, including some of his personal life is a nice touch to show these are regular people away from the field. Going above and beyond, even for a simple freelance job like this one, led to me getting asked to do more work on their website and building my network for future opportunities.

If you do quality, consistent work and take care of your clients, they will always think of you first when other needs arise. They will also be more apt to celebrate your successes with you and refer you to friends, family, and other business colleagues.

Market Yourself

As freelance writers, we cannot sit behind our computers all day and expect potential clients to find us. Legitimize yourself by starting a business, even if it's a simple sole proprietorship, and then create a website. Invest in a site that promotes you and makes you easy to find. Hire someone to build the site for you, but make sure you write the content. From there, get business cards, build an engaging social media presence, ask for referrals, and tell everyone that *you are for hire!*[4] The more you put your business in front of people, whether physically or through some form of marketing, advertising, networking, or speaking engagements, the more you will be remembered. Focus on what makes you unique. For example: Are you an award-winning writer? Are you local? What's your style, and why should that matter to clients? Make sure your portfolio is visible, so people can see your work and judge for themselves. Get people talking about you. If you do, word of mouth will spread like wildfire.

There are a million ways to market yourself, but my go-to is always social media. Why? Because everyone uses it, it's free, and people who need my services need to know I exist. Social media experts tout various high-level tips to improve your social media presence, such as paying attention to audience behavior, what's trending online, and strategically boosting posts. All of those and more are important. But from one writer to another, start with these tips:

Avoid putting your eggs in one basket. I love Facebook. I really do. But if my buddy Scott uses only LinkedIn, then how will I get him to see the blog posts I share or the videos I post if I am dominating a different platform? The easy answer is I won't. Extend your brand and unique messages to Instagram, Twitter, LinkedIn, YouTube, Pinterest, and more to engage different audiences. Brand your pages the same (company logo, colors, etc.), so people know it's you.

Promote your social media accounts. You must make it easy for people to find you. Include links to all your social media platforms on your website. Add clickable icons in your email signature—the more people who are aware of your presence, the better. You can start by connecting with friends and family and asking them to share your pages.

Ask for reviews. Speaking of promoting your social media accounts, don't forget to ask for reviews. New visitors are more likely to engage and do business with you if they can quickly see what people are saying about you and your ability to write. This is especially true if they know some of your fans personally.

Post often. What's the point of having a social media presence if you only post once per month, or not at all? In this arena, absence doesn't make the heart grow fonder. It gets you forgotten in a hurry. I'm not sure there is a magic formula that works for all social media platforms, especially for the average business owner like you and me who likely doesn't have time to post fifteen times a day. Start with quality and consistency; I try to post on all my platforms at least a few times a week, and I try my best to get the most out of each post.

Engage with your audience. I felt like I was just talking to myself when I first started posting. Over time, I've gained a decent following and can see that through likes, shares, and comments. If someone comments on your post, even if it's "I love this post," a simple thank-you reply will do the trick. If someone asks a question or sends you a private message, respond to them. Engagement, showing appreciation, and building a community keeps the conversation going and helps you build authentic relationships with those who see you as their writer.

Vary your posts, and have fun. You might be like me and post a link to your latest blog post to social media every week. Just make sure you are also varying your posts by incorporating videos, pictures, and other fun posts to spark engagement and show your personality.[5]

Don't Be a One-Trick Pony

As I've mentioned, there is nothing wrong with specializing as a writer. But if your goal is to stand out to a broader client base and get noticed as a freelance writer, no matter the situation, it'd be wise to be that writer who can help with any project. Being able to write about any industry or topic shows your range as a freelance writer and will bring more work in your direction. I'd even go so far as to say it makes you a better writer overall.[6]

As I said earlier, if you can become a pro at seeking out the story (regardless of the topic), constructing narratives that different audiences will enjoy, and consistently finding the human-interest element to draw everyone in, you instantly become extremely valuable to a lot of organizations. The same can be said if you can market yourself as both a classically trained writer *and* editor. A potential client may not necessarily need you as a writer, but if you have a sharp eye for editing and can make whatever content they are churning out look like gold, then you just became the white unicorn they've been looking for.

There are countless ways to help yourself stand out as a writer and get clients to think of you first. Hopefully, the tips I mentioned in this chapter provide a solid launching point for your writing career.

But whether you're a freelancer, a short-story writer, a journalist, or working on the next great American novel, when you set out to write, write to a purpose.

Write Like You Mean It to Be Read

12

Honoring the Editing Process

"The beautiful part of writing is that you don't have
to get it right the first time, unlike, say, a brain
surgeon. You can always do it better, find the exact
word, the apt phrase, the leaping simile."

—Robert Cormier

Through the course of this book so far, we've talked a lot about writing in general and writing in specific types of genres. We've even discussed how to be a great storyteller, the basic mechanics of writing, and how writing with the active voice materially strengthens every sentence you type. Even when you do all of that, and you have what you think is a completed piece, you must make sure it has been properly edited—both by you and an eagle-eyed editor—to smooth out the rough edges and make sure what you have truly is ready for print.

This chapter is a perfect representation of the editing process and everything it should entail, but not in the way you might think. As much as it pains me to admit, I didn't include this chapter in the first draft of this book. I know! Crazy, right? I focused so much on talking to writers about writing that somehow, I didn't even think about going into more detail about editing until the very end as I cobbled together a quick reference section. Talk about not honoring the editing process! That'd be like making Michael Jordan a footnote in a documentary on the greatest basketball players of all time.

I'll chalk the oversight up to being a first-timer at writing my own book. But my lack of foresight was both moronic and ironic since I had been carefully editing and fine-tuning my thoughts and words the entire time. I also sent a rough draft (sans this chapter) to a handful of friends and colleagues for honest feedback. One of the first messages I got back was from another writer, who carefully said, "I liked it. But I kept waiting for you to talk about editing—and it never came."

He was 100 percent correct. Just as Jordan is synonymous with basketball and Serena Williams is synonymous with tennis, editing is a massive part of the writing process. You can't have one without the other. Therefore, I believe all writers must know how to edit their own writing, help others edit theirs, and, whenever possible, have a stable of editors watching their back to catch anything that was missed.

Your editor is more than just a glorified spell-checker. They are the last line of defense in quality writing. In this chapter, let's dive into a few key points and helpful tips to help you understand what it means to honor the editing process.

What Editing Is and What It Includes

Editing is a critical stage of the writing process, where the goal of the writer or editor is to read something intended to be published and improve it by fixing anything that can make it better. This includes catching spelling and grammatical errors, making sentences clearer, fact-checking, pointing out holes or missing elements to a story, and more. Editing is an ongoing process that starts with the writer, who should be editing their work as much as possible, and ends with handing the piece over to someone else—or several someone elses—as an "extra set of eyes."

You can break the editing process down into a few crucial categories depending on your specific needs, though there is also a ton of overlap.

Development. When you edit or ask someone to edit your work, you're improving its overall quality and preparing it for publication. You're reworking entire sentences and paragraphs for improved flow, clarity, and readability. You're also catching typos, style inconsistencies, and other obvious errors. Overall, an editor reads objectively to point out potential issues.

Copy editing. Think of a copy editor as quality control. They can do all the same things as a general editor, but their job is to ensure the document they are looking at is factually accurate and stylistically consistent with the way certain things are done at whatever publication you are writing for. If you didn't spell out "University of North Texas" on the first reference or weren't sure whether to spell out a number or leave it as a numeral, a copy editor is going to catch these issues and fix them. They'll also eliminate clichés and word repetition.

Proofreading. Proofreading is taking an article that is considered "final" and providing a last-minute sweep for grammar and spelling errors. When I am proofreading documents for clients, I'm ensuring all punctuation is perfect and there are no misuses of words (did you mean "flyer" or "flier"?)

or extra spaces between words. I'm double-checking formatting and if the document is stylistically consistent from start to finish.[1]

These editing processes shape our writing. Sometimes, they may only involve a few minor tweaks here and there. Other times, they can mean a complete rewrite. The result is hopefully a written piece that is error-free, accurate, easy to read, and something you can be proud of.

Is It Wrong to Start a Sentence with "And" or "But"?

As far back as I can remember, I was told that it's wrong to start a sentence with "and" or "but." The funny thing is that I was never given a good reason why. I'm here to tell you that it is perfectly acceptable to start a sentence with "and" or "but." Just like anything else, you never want to overuse the privilege. But, if the situation calls for it, why not? Starting a sentence with a coordinating conjunction has the following benefits:

- **Your writing is easier to read.**
- **You can break up long sentences.**
- **You achieve a certain style or tone.**
- **Your writing becomes more impactful.**

Here are a few examples of starting a sentence with "and," "but," or other conjunctions:

- *Can I start a sentence with a conjunction? And can you read this when I'm done?*
- *Mike wasn't feeling well. Yet he still got on the Zoom call.*
- *John could take the trash out and empty the dishwasher for his wife. Or he could do both of those things and also take her out for a nice dinner.*
- *Alicia turned in her math test first. But she forgot to put her name on it.[5]*

Why You Need Someone Else to Edit Your Work

I've leaned on plenty of quality editors over the years to help make what I'm writing better. Whether it was Scott Parks, the copy desk at the newspapers and magazines I've written for, other writers, or close friends, they all played a significant role. But let's go back to Scott for a second because throughout that entire stretch from 2014 to when I left the *Denton Record-Chronicle* in 2018 to do Edit This full time, there were very few days where I wasn't in his office asking him to read a rough draft. I simply didn't feel comfortable pushing forward on something unless I had at least shown it to Scott at some point during the process. In fact, that quickly became a running joke in the newsroom between me and a few of my cohorts: "Did you show it to Scott yet?"

I wanted to do more than write. I wanted to take my editing game to the next level—to be able to look at my work and what others wrote with the same critical eye that Scott had. I remember sitting in his office one day for over an hour as he critiqued everything I wrote on an article about NFL offensive lineman Daryl Williams. Daryl was a local athlete who made it big and was about to play in the Super Bowl for the Carolina Panthers. Scott dissected everything from the words I chose to pointing out things that I missed and asking me why I thought this story was a good idea in the first place. He questioned everything, even the stuff I thought was obvious.

Some of the guys in the office grimaced at the thought of being stuck with Scott for that long, but I enjoyed it. His critiques made me better at writing.

All writers need a good editor. It doesn't matter if you are a rookie or a veteran, a student or a teacher, or simply someone who likes to write on the side. We all make mistakes. We could edit our work a dozen times on our own and still likely miss something. So don't hesitate to step aside and let someone—a friend, parent, spouse, coworker, or your own personal Scott Parks—be your editor.

If you don't, you'll fall into four main booby traps of solely relying on yourself:

Bogging down your creative flow. Being your own writer and editor is inefficient 100 percent of the time and a recipe for disaster because it bogs down your creative flow. If you're going to do both, write first and then edit. And then give it to someone you trust for the final edit.

A lack of objectivity. Quality writers should be invested in their work. Whether it's a long feature article or a short blog post, it's still *your* baby. But we all need someone to objectively look at our work to point out potential issues. The more attached you are, the less objective you are as an editor. Someone else can come in with a new perspective.

Tired eyes. Have you ever spent hours painting a bedroom, and your spouse walks in and immediately points out several spots where the paint roller didn't quite do its job? How come you didn't see that first? It's because you've been looking at it for too long. Fresh eyes mean a world of difference. An editor, even if it's a friend from down the street who isn't a professional, is sure to catch *something* you've missed—whether that something is a typo, a run-on sentence, or a potentially story-ruining inconsistency.

Missing out on growth opportunities. I fancy myself a clean writer, but I wouldn't be where I am today without some great editors by my side. I can't tell you how many times the copy desk has caught errors or called me to suggest a better way of writing a sentence. I want to grow as a writer, so I crave that communication. But there are writers out there who are too afraid to have their work criticized. As a result, they won't grow. Their articles will always leave something to be desired, their books won't sell, and if they are a freelance writer, they will run the risk of losing out on writing opportunities.[2]

How It's Still Possible to Edit Your Own Work

Never edit your own writing. That's what writers, students, and small-business owners hear all the time—at least from the standpoint of relying solely on yourself. At some point, after you've self-edited, you need to give the piece to someone else.

But what if having someone edit your writing isn't an option?

What if you need something written and published now, and no one is available?

What if you procrastinated and now you don't have time to seek a second opinion?

What if you're stubborn and just prefer to edit your own writing?

While trying to edit your own writing for style, tone, structure, and substance isn't ideal, it's not impossible. So if you prefer to edit your own writing or don't have a choice in the matter, here are six tips to ensure what you publish is the best it can possibly be.[3]

Read out loud. So many errors with sentence structure, wordiness, and grammar can be fixed by reading your work out loud. If I find myself stumbling over big words or running out of breath reading a long sentence out loud, then I know it's time for edits.

Edit in a different format. Print the article and use a red pen to make edits. If on your laptop, change the text size, font, and color or convert from Word to PDF. If you're writing a blog post, copy and paste it into the program you're publishing it in.

Walk away. Write, and then let it sit for a few hours, overnight, or a few days. Your brain gets a reset so you can transition easily from writer to editor. When you come back, you're likely to notice misspellings, confusing jargon, and inconsistencies.

Edit in smaller steps. It can be difficult trying to read for grammar, sentence structure, flow, and wordiness all at once. Break the editing process up into manageable steps by checking only for mistakes, then grammar, and then wordiness. If you're editing a book, edit a few chapters at a time, and then take a break.

Three Grammar Rules I Don't Mind Breaking

Grammar rules make everything we write clear, uniform, professional, and easy to understand. But some are old and way too stilted for the world we live in now. These old grammar rules can be broken from time to time or, at a minimum, bent to meet our needs:

- **Using contractions.** There's nothing grammatically wrong with contractions, but you also have to know your audience. If you're in the world of academia or are writing in a more formal setting, then yes, avoid using them. For nearly everyone else, contractions make writing conversational, friendly, accessible, and easier to read.
- **Two spaces between sentences.** Nothing says "showing your age" more than using two spaces between sentences. Most of us old-timers who regularly used typewriters remember spacing twice after each sentence to clearly define the end of one sentence and the start of another. Most fonts and programs today adjust characters for us, making the "double space" unnecessary.
- **Ending a sentence with a preposition.** It is better to avoid ending a sentence with a preposition (with, to, on, in, at, of, etc.). But I also argue that, in many cases, it makes complete sense to break this rule if it helps us avoid confusing or awkward writing. For example, would you prefer to write, "From where did this ball come?" No, you'd write, "Where did this ball come from?"[6]

Read in reverse. Though tedious, this is a great tactic to help you edit your own writing. Instead of reading each paragraph front to back, reverse it and see what happens.

There's an app for that. If you can't have someone read and edit your work, at least invest in one of many editor applications. Grammarly is a great proofreading tool, and I swear by it.[4]

Here's a final thought on honoring the editing process. There are people out there who are "just writers." There are others who are "just editors." And that's all well and fine. They have a specialty, and they're sticking to it. Still, anyone who takes the time to be a trained writer and editor instantly places themselves in a more favorable position. Not only will your writing improve, but you'll be looked at to take on more difficult assignments before anyone else. Why? Because your boss or client believes in you. You'll be able to craft first drafts that are clean and closer to being publication ready by the time your editor gets ahold of it.

And last but not least: for the freelancers out there, if you are both a writer and editor, more opportunities will present themselves beyond writing-only gigs or editing-only assignments. I write for a particular magazine, and not only am I one of their lead writers, but I'm also the editor for all of their monthly publications. Talk about doubling your income—and all it took was spending more time honoring the editing process.

13

Marketing Your Work

"Tactics without strategy is the noise before defeat."

—Sun Tzu

If you are a young writer who wants to get your work beyond the spiral notebook or laptop file it's in right now and into the hands of avid readers, literary agents, publishers, writers, and perhaps even store shelves everywhere, it would behoove you to learn everything you can about marketing. Because at this point, especially after you and your editor have smoothed out the rough edges of your piece, you should feel even more confident to start seeking people out who might be interested in your stuff. The most basic definition of marketing is the act or business of promoting and selling a product or service. That may not feel like it pertains to writers, but it does! We are promoting ourselves as writers and authors—as the experts of our craft. We are promoting our writing, which is really good and deserves to see the light of day. Writing and marketing go hand in hand, whether you write books, poetry, articles for newspapers and magazines, or a weekly blog. Marketing your work takes effort and time, but thankfully, it's a pretty straightforward concept:

1. Write something people will enjoy.
2. Get it in front of those people.

If you've made it this far in my book, you should know how to write something people enjoy. Like a soldier who gutted his or her way through basic training and has been issued all the standard combat gear and weaponry, you are now armed with the necessary tools, tips, tricks, and life hacks to not only write like you mean it but also write like you mean it to be read. You just need a strategy to get your work in front of the right people and to promote it in the right places. By the end of this chapter, you'll have some ideas on how to do that in the way that makes the most sense for whatever it is that you are writing.

Start by Knowing Your Audience

Many young writers—and maybe a few veteran ones too—think that they don't have to worry about marketing their stuff until *after* they've finished writing. If you think about it, though, marketing your work starts the second you know what you want to write and before you pick up a pen and start writing. After all, you're writing to a specific audience, right? This means everything you do moving forward—the words you use, your tone, the topic, the characters you create, how you form your argument, the stories you tell, the problems you solve, how you set the scene, how technical you get—is all based on attracting, appeasing, and wowing a specific audience. That's marketing in a nutshell. If you take your audience into consideration before you start writing, your work will be set up for success in the market. If you ignore your audience, identify the wrong audience, or speak to too broad an audience, you will find it increasingly more difficult to gain traction as a writer and to have your writing seen. So in thinking about marketing your work, the first question you should ask yourself—besides "What do I want to write about?"—is "Who is my audience?" You can get technical and consider factors such as age, sex, education level, economic status, or values. Or you can think in more general terms. Consider these examples:

The Harry Potter series wasn't marketed specifically to men over fifty. I mean, maybe there are men over fifty who like Harry Potter, but really, J. K. Rowling was writing to and creating a world for youth and fantasy fiction lovers.

On the completely opposite end of the spectrum, there is the popular blog *The Penny Hoarder*. This blog serves an audience interested in personal finance. Every post is targeted toward people who want to learn more about making and saving money, budgeting, retirement, eliminating debt, and so on. Everything they write serves that audience. Anything outside of that would not perform well within that audience.

Smaller community newspapers with a circulation size of thirty-five thousand or less focus on hyper-local content (such as local government, entertainment, community feel-good pieces, high school sports, and school district and university news). Will they have a few national news pieces from time to time? Yes. But the audience that subscribes to that paper wouldn't come to them for national AP news anyway. They want to know what's going on in their neighborhood, and that's what they expect to read about.

This book, *Write Like You Mean It*, is for writers. That's a broad audience, so I had to make sure I spoke directly to every writing community and writers of all experience levels and interests. Had I promised a book for writers but completely ignored fiction and nonfiction writers, the entire concept would fall short.

Knowing your audience is also critical in editing. Once you've defined your audience and written what you think is quality content, you must go back with a fine-tooth comb and make sure what you've written makes sense for who you are writing to. Are you writing to physicians or patients? Are you targeting kids or adults? Do you see how your answer to either of those questions can alter how you go about editing your work and making it as good as it can possibly be?

If you know, understand, cater to, and anticipate your audience from the outset, you'll be ahead of the game in terms of marketing your work. Keeping them in mind throughout the writing *and* editing process ensures you will have a marketable piece when the dust settles.

What You Should Do with Your Work Once It's Finished

Once you have identified your audience and created some really compelling material that speaks to who you are as a writer, you have to start thinking about getting it out there in the most effective way possible. This is not a time to guess or push forward with some sort of haphazard strategy. This is your work. You worked extremely hard on it, and it deserves the grandest stage possible. So as you move forward, with writing in hand and hope in your heart, remember the following:

Be mindful of where you're promoting your work. I get it; you're excited about getting your work out there. But you have to be choosy with where you go with it so that you maximize your marketing opportunities and get it in front of the right audience. Keep in mind during your marketing efforts that there are hundreds upon hundreds of publications, publishers, forums, and online media. Not all of them specialize in what you are writing. Not all of them are looking for what you are writing about. Not all of them are the best fit. If you're writing a literary short story or poem, for example, approaching a local or national newspaper probably isn't your best bet. The same can be said if you try to bring a New Age piece to a conservative media outlet. Do your research and seek out the best landing spots for your material. Targeting the ones that match your writing topics, style, and goals can get you in front of your audience. You'll have more success and be more efficient with your time if you do.

Create a website. Not having a website equals invisibility in a tech-driven age. So while I mentioned websites earlier, it bears repeating. All writers need a website these days, and many can be built on the cheap through DIY sites like Wix, Weebly, and Squarespace. Doing so helps you build legitimacy in the marketplace as a writer and creates the perfect landing spot to share your portfolio for published and nonpublished material with a simple web link. A word of caution that I want to throw out there, though, is to be careful with the DIY sites mentioned above. There isn't anything wrong with going that route (my website is through Wix)—just be sure you take your time and make the site look and feel as professional as it possibly can. Write your own content, use the right keywords to help with search engine optimization, and design it so that it's user friendly. I recommend hiring a website designer if your budget allows. If you can't afford one, start with something small and then upgrade as quickly as possible. A website designer can help with customization, give you more space to tell your story and share your work, and give you someone to turn to when your site crashes. A website is working for you twenty-four seven, even when you're busy writing away into the wee hours of the morning.

Network, schmooze, and learn. You need to get out from behind your computer, whether you are done with your latest masterpiece or not. Put yourself in a position where you are either always in front of your target audience or in front of people who can get you in front of your target audience and entities who are looking for new writers. Networking events are big, even if you're the only writer in the room. This happens to me more often than not—I am almost always the only writer at a morning chamber meeting or networking group, and I see this as a good thing. You never know who knows who, if you'll bump into a literary agent, or if the plumber a few tables over happens to be married to the CEO of a local magazine. Business organizations are promoting networking groups all the time. Universities host writing conferences and workshops. Bookstores host book signings and other events. They are easy to find, so be there as much as you can. Another element that falls into this tip are speaking engagements. I started doing these several years ago—nothing big; maybe fifteen or twenty people. But in speaking about my craft and a specific topic that interested them, I was able to build relationships, network with the right audience, and set myself up as an authority. When you've got a book, an article, or a short story that you're trying to get out into the world, schmoozing and constantly looking for ways to soak in new information helps.

Join a writing forum or community. When you're just starting out as a writer, you may find yourself sitting at a coffee shop by yourself—a lot. But to have the best chance of success, you need to get yourself around other writers—at writing conferences, workshops, online writing communities and forums, and any place you can. Online writing communities and forums are all over the web, are easily accessible, and are a great place to learn a lot of interesting marketing tricks and techniques from seasoned pros. Utilize these communities to beef up your beta reader list to catch issues with your manuscript and to give and receive support and encouragement, reviews, and more. Writers want to be around other writers. It's just that simple. We can learn a lot from each other, especially when it comes to marketing yourself and your material.

Social media. Just like every writer needs a website, every writer needs a social media presence. So if you don't have one, get one. Facebook is a great place to build relationships and share your work. But make it separate from your personal page. In other words, create a business page, even if it's also under your author name. The same goes for LinkedIn, Instagram, Pinterest, and other social media channels. Create a YouTube channel and promote your work and other tricks of the trade through video. You'll build communities across a variety of mediums, and that will help get your name and work out there.

Have a blog. A blog that is consistently maintained and has plenty of value-adding content keeps readers updated on your work and establishes you in the writing world. I've had a writing- and editing-related blog on my Edit This website for several years. Before that, I was using Blogger.com to get my writing into the public eye. I am diligent about posting in my current blog every week. I credit that consistency to landing me several opportunities that I wouldn't normally have, especially when it comes to meeting new business partners such as website designers, graphic artists, and everyday business owners who are looking for writers. If they haven't seen the post, someone is sharing it with them. Blogging consistently has also put me in a position to take many of those tips and stories that I'm writing about and use them to write my first book. The chapters I wrote on writer's block and how using a pen and paper first can be good for writers initially started out as blog posts. Blogging has also allowed me to share my creative side, spark engagement, fine-tune my writing, and put my work in front of people who enjoy reading it and might ask me to write for them.

Do the little things to promote yourself. Get yourself a few hundred business cards, create a professional email address (for example, steve@editthisllc.com), and get rid of the silly one you created when you were seventeen. Use your email signature line to highlight all the ways people can find you (social media links, phone numbers, website addresses, etc.). Make a big deal out of any awards you've won, especially if they were on a state or national level. The little things matter, and if you pay attention to them, they will pay dividends as you go out into the world.

At the end of the day, sitting behind a computer screen pumping out quality writing and dreaming about being a published writer is only going to get you so far—and not published. At some point, you have to get up and market your work. You owe it to yourself to give your writing a chance to see the light of day. And it doesn't have to be rocket science. Use some of the tips above, change them up at your discretion so that they work best for you, and get to work.

A Few Networking Tips

Not all of us are versed in the ways of networking, especially when we've never done it before. Here are a few ways to help you feel more comfortable in that setting:

- **Have your business cards handy.** One of the first questions someone will ask you at a networking event (besides your name) is, "What do you do for a living?" Don't leave them hanging! Have plenty of cards in your wallet, purse, or pockets.
- **Have a good elevator speech ready.** Regardless of whether you are a networking pro or not, you need to have a quick and succinct explanation of who you are, what your business is, and what you do. Keep it simple and appealing, and the questions will start rolling in as they are eager to learn more.
- **Look approachable.** Smile, stand up straight, look interested in everything that's going on around you. Even if you don't know what to say, be nice, and let whomever you are talking to take the wheel at first.
- **Don't go alone.** There's no rule that says you have to go alone to a networking event! Inviting a friend or a family member can help take the pressure off.
- **Don't hang out in one spot.** I know that cheese tray looks tasty, but it's not a good idea to stand by the buffet line the entire night. Move around and mingle—this is your chance to talk about your business and writing career!

14

Getting Published

"I think new writers everywhere need
opportunities to get published."

—Greg Egan

If you want to be a professional writer, the goal of everything you do is to be published. And I want to reiterate that "getting published" isn't a term specific to book writers. I'm speaking to all writers, regardless of whether you are an aspiring journalist looking for your first byline, a blogger hoping to gain more followers and go mainstream, a feature writer eager to catch on with a few magazines, a first-time novelist, or a writer with a niche somewhere in between. As I said before, to *write like you mean it* also means to write like you mean it *to be read*. It takes persistence, lots of writing, and a healthy dose of luck, but the good news is that new writers are getting published every single day. Veteran writers are venturing out into different arenas and finding just as much success. If you've got the talent, passion, and drive, there's no reason you can't be one of them.

I still remember the first time I got published. It was my sophomore year in college, and I was assigned an investigative piece for the *NT Daily* on the football program's declining fan attendance at home games. I recall the first moment I saw my byline and feeling my heart swell with pride. That was *my* name on that article. I worked hard on it and even held my own in a boardroom interview with several bigwigs from the athletics department. The main image on the story was a caricature of a fan sitting by himself in an empty section of the stands. He had a foam finger in one hand and a blank expression on his face. It was perfect, just like the story that followed. In the grand scheme of things, it was the student newspaper and not the *New York Times*. But it was a publication nonetheless—and something I could add to my portfolio. People would read that article. Hopefully, they'd enjoy it. More importantly, it marked the start of my career as a writer. That following summer, I was offered a job at a small newspaper, and I've had the good fortune of having my writing published thousands of times since—in newspapers, magazines, newsletters, online, and now in a book. I've unapologetically celebrated all of those opportunities as if I had just buried an off-balance jumper with no time left on the clock in game seven of the NBA Finals. It never gets old seeing my stuff in print, and you deserve to experience the same excitement for yours.

For the next few pages, I'm going to share with you a few publishing options that every writer should consider, and even the pros and cons for a few of them. We are also going to talk about rejection—because . . . well . . . it comes with the territory—and the importance of keeping your eye on the prize. In closing, we're going to talk about what we've learned in this book, take a trip down memory lane, and pull out a few takeaways.

I hate to refer to the final section of this chapter as the conclusion because, ironically, it symbolizes the start of your writing career, not the end. But this book does have to end somewhere. Thankfully, we're not there quite yet, so let's enjoy the last few moments we have. You're done writing, and you've marketed yourself and your work to the best of your ability—here are a few publishing options.

Traditionally Publishing Books

Before there were options like self-publishing and hybrid publishing, traditional publishing was the only way to get your book into the market. Even today, this is what many writers imagine when they think about getting published. You as the author submit your manuscript to the publisher, and the publisher pays you for the rights to publish the work. There are hundreds of publishing companies out there. Penguin Random House and HarperCollins are two of them. There's also Thomson Reuters, Hachette, and Macmillan. The trick is persuading them to accept your work. Unless you're already a big name, it's not as easy to get the publisher's attention, and there are several steps you have to take to put yourself in that position. The first step is to find an agent to shop your manuscript around. Why do you need a literary agent? Well, while you most certainly can get published without one, let's just say it's far less likely. Literary agents are gatekeepers to the most prestigious publishers in the world. They get you in the front door, and oftentimes, the publisher will only want to talk to the literary agent first to see if your manuscript is worth the investment. Finding the right one takes time and plenty of good old-fashioned research, but several go-to sites include AgentQuery.com, PublishersMarketplace.com, and QueryTracker.net. When you're looking for an agent, pick someone who has experience with your genre and has a good track record in terms of whom he or she has sold to and how recently. Most of this information can be found in their bio, on their website, or through a phone or in-person consultation if you get that far. Once you've found an agent that you feel comfortable with, give them a strong book proposal and a few sample chapters (in some cases, you'll need the full manuscript) to see if they'll take your assignment on. Once you've found an agent, they will be committed to helping you sell your book to the traditional publisher that is right for you.

Publishing Books with a Hybrid Company

I had never heard of hybrid publishing prior to jumping into getting this book published. While it does not work for everyone, it is a fast-growing option for book writers who want the red-carpet treatment for their book. Brown Books Publishing Group in Dallas, Texas, for example, combines all the retail access and advantages of traditional publishing (editing, cover design, warehousing, marketing, etc.) with the profitability and creative control of self-publishing. Authors are involved in the creative process and get the support they need to have the best book they can possibly have without giving up the rights to their work. Granted, hybrid publishing has upfront production-related costs, meaning that the financial risk falls largely on the author rather than the publishing house. But on the back end, assuming the book is successful, the author enjoys much higher royalty rates per sale. There are hybrid publishers all over the country. Noteworthy hybrid companies besides Brown Books include TCK Publishing, Abuzz Press, Boyle & Dalton Publishing, and Greenleaf Book Group.

Self-Publishing Books

If you've got one or a few books waiting to be published, you might not need to "wow" a literary agent, meander your way through several gatekeepers, or hope and pray a big publishing house like Penguin Random House sees your work as a pot of gold. Self-publishing puts the power to publish into your hands, and it has had an enormous impact on the publishing industry with the rise of smart devices, e-books, online subscriptions, and the ever-changing behaviors of avid readers worldwide. Many highly successful authors—Christopher Paolini and E. L. James come to mind—began their journey by going the self-publishing route and became ridiculously successful. There are many advantages, the biggest of which is that self-publishing is faster. Publishing through a big-box house could take six to eighteen months—assuming they like what you have—and could involve spending money that you do not have. With self-publishing, you can theoretically finish your book today in a very cheap way and publish it online tomorrow through Kindle Direct Publishing. I interviewed one young lady for a separate magazine article about her experience. She was a junior in high school and literally got her book on KDP with the click of a mouse while surrounded by her family. Now, she's a published author—as a teenager. Self-publishing can mean better royalties, control over the product, and a potentially longer shelf life. Just make sure it's the right option for you. There is no editorial and marketing support with self-publishing. While that can save you time and get you published faster, your copy could be riddled with mistakes that you didn't spot on your own, and you don't have anyone helping you avoid plot holes or suggesting new elements that can make your book more appealing to readers. No one is helping you with your book title, book cover, or book signings or putting your book in front of your target audience consistently. It's all on you. If you're writing a small children's book, maybe these cons won't impact you at all. But they could if you're writing a textbook or educational piece that needs more exposure. Clearly, self-publishing is not without its challenges. But with more than two million authors published on KDP alone (not even factoring in other self-publishing sites), the opportunity is there.

Self-Publishing Short-Form Work

The self-publishing world isn't just for book writers. Those of you who like to write poems, feature stories, and blogs can self-publish, too, and this is particularly important when it comes to building your portfolio. Publishers and editors at newspapers, magazines, blogging sites, and other online outlets prefer to see and read what you've had published, but not all of them have a track record of being willing to publish new and aspiring writers. So getting the attention of the big boys requires a little ingenuity in seeking out ways to either self-publish or find someone who is willing to support your budding career. Thankfully, the internet has made it incredibly easy for young writers to get a few quick bylines. Here are a few ways to do that (online or in print):

Write for your college paper. Granted, not everyone goes to college or was in college to be a writer. But if you are a student and are there to write, the college paper is a great way to get regular bylines. They are organized and structured just like a big paper, with different sections of interest, a website in some cases, a copy desk, and thousands of on-campus readers. And if you write for them long enough, it will be an easy springboard into getting hired to write for metro newspapers or local magazines.

Create your own blog. Sites like WordPress, Blogger, Wix, and others are excellent platforms for starting a free online presence and creating links to your self-published work. Blogging puts the power of getting published into your hands, and you can end up developing quite an audience if you keep at it.

Guest post on someone else's blog. This isn't exactly a self-publishing tactic, but when you're just starting out, you also have to think of self-publishing as putting yourself in a position to be published with other people. This can be as simple as writing a piece and reaching out to some of your favorite bloggers to see if the topic works for what they typically write about. Maybe they will throw you a bone and add you as a regular guest poster. The only way you'll know is if you ask.

Find a digital publishing platform. Medium is one of many popular free publishing sites where you can get your stand-alone pieces or blogs published within minutes and reach a growing audience of nearly two hundred million readers. Medium is just one option. There is a labyrinth of quality publishing platforms out there, including LinkedIn and EzineArticles. Try one or self-publish on several, and see what happens. While not every site works for every writer, they are a good place to get published. And as I mentioned in chapter 13, look for where the people you are trying to reach hang out online. That's where to publish.

Publishing in Newspapers and Magazines

Publishing is a lot easier when you already work full time for a newspaper or magazine. Stories are assigned, others fall into your lap, and it's easier to get your editor's attention when you want to pitch a story idea. When you're a young writer who is looking for that first publishing opportunity, you need to get on everyone's radar.

Call or email. Publishers of newspapers and magazines always want to have a deep pool of potential writers who can help them churn out the content that matters most to their readers. Express interest and get on their list by calling or emailing to let them know who you are and what you specialize in, and show them the work that you've done. You may be able to get your foot in the door as an intern and build a portfolio that way.

Pitch story ideas. Many magazines will take submitted content if it meshes with what their readers would enjoy. When you're trying to break into the world of publishing for newspapers and magazines, don't be afraid to pitch timely, useful story ideas.

Keep writing. Just because you're not getting a callback doesn't mean you have to stop writing. Keep writing, and keep reaching out to other entities. Even if they aren't biting now, that doesn't mean someone else won't.

Be Mindful of Where You Try to Get Published

Once you feel confident in your writing skills and want to pursue something more meaningful, make sure you aren't wasting your time pursuing a publishing source that doesn't match your goals. Too many times, writers get fixated on impressing the people they think hold the key to publishing their work when they should be making sure those entities are the right fit to begin with. What I mean is that different places have different specialties, specific audiences, and different styles. Just like they want to find the right writer or author for their needs, you as a writer or author must ensure they are meeting your needs. It simply makes sense, and doing so will likely get you published faster. For example, I chose Brown Books to help me with this book. I did so for a variety of reasons, but the biggest selling point was that they attract a general audience. They publish a little bit of everything, but they're also very selective in that process and offer a hybrid service that has flipped the script on what many people know as the traditional publishing realm. Having done my research and looked at the options available to me, I knew immediately that if they liked my manuscript, they'd be invested in making sure my book was a success.

The same can be said for my life as a magazine writer. I know that every story idea I pitch to one particular client has to meet their standard for meaningful hyper-local content. Sports stories about the World Series probably won't catch their attention, but if I told them a former high school standout from their community is about to pitch game three, that's a better story. By the same token, if I have a great story on a local business owner who thrived during the COVID-19 pandemic by making and selling reusable cloth face masks, then it's more likely that they'll give me the green light to write it for them.

A Few Quick Thoughts on Rejection

No one wants to be rejected, especially when you are pouring your heart and soul into a career you want so badly but can't seem to get going in the right direction. Sadly, rejection is part of the process of getting published—and almost everyone who has been published has been rejected a few times. Best-sellers like Stephen King's *Carrie*, Mary Shelley's *Frankenstein*, George Orwell's *Animal Farm*, and J. K. Rowling's original manuscript for *Harry Potter* were reportedly rejected dozens of times by different publishing houses. Perhaps Stephen King has the best response to rejection: "By the time I was fourteen the nail in my wall would no longer support the weight of the rejection slips impaled upon it. I replaced the nail with a spike and went on writing." If someone like Stephen King can be unfazed by that many rejections, so can you. So can I. What we also have to realize is that there are countless factors that go into why writing is rejected. Sometimes it is legitimately horrible or has too many grammar and spelling errors, but many times, it's not that at all. The publisher could have way too many submissions to sift through at the moment. Perhaps they aren't accepting submissions in the genre you've written in or the topic you've written about at all right now. Maybe you just didn't follow the submission directions, or your writing doesn't feel timely to the publication. Sometimes, rejection isn't about you at all—some publications only want to work with certain writers. And sometimes, your writing isn't bad, but it's just not quite good enough either.

If a publisher has told you no, the best thing that can happen is that you get a very specific rejection letter with the reasons why. While it may feel like a dagger to the heart if it has to do with your writing, this is the publisher's way of telling you to keep improving your work and not stop trying to get published. Like Stephen King said, keep on writing. Stay positive and never second-guess your place at the proverbial writer's table. Accept criticism, strive to improve on your writing at all costs, and look in the right places for opportunities. Sooner or later, you will get published.

Write Like You Mean It!

It's funny how much a book can change as you are writing it. When I first sat down and started typing, I thought I knew exactly how to attack this project. Sure, I had never written a book before. But so what? I've been published thousands of times in other arenas, I have a successful writing and editing business where I've helped others write their books, and I have a genuine desire to create a so-called "self-help book for writers." How hard could it be? I'm a writer. I've been in nearly every writer's shoes. Thus, I have plenty to talk about. All I had to do was type. I created a "fail-safe" list of chapters, and as I wrote, my confidence began to soar. "Wow," I said to myself at one point. "This is some really good stuff!" I finished the rough draft, sent it out to friends for feedback, and all of my initial thoughts about how good this book was were immediately validated. I found a publisher. I thought I was good to go.

As it turns out, what I had was nothing more than a really strong start.

Those who read those earlier iterations will tell you this final version is completely different in terms of size, scope, purpose, flow, and functionality. It's clearer. It's more concise. The rough edges have been smoothed out. Additional chapters were added to make sure I was speaking to *all* writers. It was hard work—harder than I ever imagined. But I'm proud. I'm proud because not only does this represent my passion for the written word, but it's a perfect metaphor for who we all are as writers. When you're just starting out, and even as you get twenty or thirty years down the line, you think you've reached a point where you have it all figured out—just like I thought with this book. People tell you that you're good, you learn to decipher between what is and is not quality writing, and you push forward thinking that you've got it all under control. Then you realize through an epiphany or an editor clubbing you upside the head that you don't know near enough. Being a writer is a tedious, lifelong endeavor where there are always rough edges to smooth out. There's room to improve, and this book is proof of that. My hope is that the final version—although I still wish I could have written it better—makes you just as proud to be a writer as it makes me.

There are so many takeaways that I hope you hold on to after reading this book, but if you don't remember anything else, remember these things:

- **Don't let your fears get in the way of pursuing your passion. You were born to write.**
- **Be intentional about mastering the active voice and basic mechanics of good writing.**
- **Writer's block is not the enemy; it's trying to make you better. Embrace that mindset.**
- **Stay organized, and always keep your audience in mind.**
- **Be a storyteller.**
- **Be receptive to feedback, and build yourself a trusted writing community.**
- **Read, read, read. There is always something to learn from good and bad writing.**
- **Strive to write each sentence better than you did yesterday.**
- **Get out from behind your computer and market yourself and your work.**
- **Unapologetically celebrate every opportunity you have to be published!**

I am eternally committed to being a valuable resource to anyone who wants to be a better writer. It sounds overplayed, but we writers need to stick together. It's the reason why I wrote this book.

I am living my dream as a writer. Now, it's your turn.

Write like you mean it!

Acknowledgments

So many people played a part in me writing this book that I can't possibly thank all of them. That's such a cliché statement, but it's true!

Thank you, Ed and Maureen, my amazing parents, who not only encouraged me to shoot for the stars but also made umpteen million sacrifices to set me up for success. To my clients, practically all of whom have become dear friends over the years—thank you for trusting me to capture your voice with my writing and for supporting me as I chase this dream career.

Thank you to all the writers, editors, and bosses (past and present) in my life. Whether it was because you gave me my big break, made my writing better, allowed me to mentor you, challenged me, encouraged me, knocked me down a notch, or told me to delete everything and start all over again, I am a better writer and person because of you.

Christian and Jackson, the greatest joy in my life is to be your dad. Always believe in yourself, chase your dreams, and be good people. And to my wife, Leslie: you're my rock and biggest fan, and I can never possibly repay you. I love you.

And finally, thank you from the bottom of my heart to the team at Brown Books Publishing Group for not only taking a chance on a new author but also helping to make this book the best it can possibly be.

References and Resources for Further Reading

Edit This, LLC (EditThisLLC.com)

A useful writing and editing service for individuals and small businesses, Edit This also publishes a weekly blog post that caters to anyone who loves the written word and wants to be better at writing. This includes helpful tips on everything from grammar to starting a blog, tackling writer's block, creative writing, and down-to-earth storytelling.

Grammarly (Grammarly.com)

This is your free online writing assistant. Using technology and natural language processing, Grammarly helps you write mistake-free content regardless of whether it's an article, book, assignment for class, email, or social media post.

Poynter (Poynter.org)

An ongoing resource blog for writers and journalists that teaches and inspires writing professionals to sharpen their skills and elevate their storytelling through ethics and fact-checking, reporting tips, and much more.

Scrivener (LiteratureAndLatte.com)

Scrivener is a word-processing software tool that helps authors of all types get their best ideas out from a spiral notebook and onto an easy-to-use platform that also helps you organize and manage all of your research, chapters, concepts, and notes.

The *AP Stylebook* (APStylebook.com)

A must-have for journalists all over the world. The *AP Stylebook* ensures you are adhering to your organization's style and usage as you craft compelling content.

The *Chicago Manual of Style* (ChicagoManualOfStyle.org)

Unlike the *AP Stylebook*, *CMOS* is the universal style and usage guide for authors, editors, and publishers of books, periodicals, and journals.

Roget's Super Thesaurus (Roget.org)

A super helpful reference tool and time-saver that helps all writers find the right words they are looking for to add color and creativity to every written piece. The latest edition costs only about twenty dollars and should be included in every writer's toolbox.

Grammar Girl (QuickAndDirtyTips.com/grammar-girl)
A fun and engaging site that regularly produces content on all things grammar, punctuation, creative ways to use the English language, and more. Ever wondered when to use a semicolon or understand the difference between "reign" and "rein"? This is your site.

Poets & Writers (PW.org)
Home to a broad range of resources for writers, including tips on how to publish and promote your writing, access to literary agent and magazine databases, writing contests, grants and awards, writer retreats, review outlets, and more.

Wattpad (Wattpad.com)
A simple, easy-to-use online community for writers who want to read, write new content, explore ways to fine-tune their craft, and more. Wattpad boasts a global community of roughly eighty million readers and writers.

Jane Friedman (JaneFriedman.com)
Jane Friedman is an accomplished writer, publisher, blogger, and author. And that's just a quick synopsis. Her website is a go-to source for publishing in the digital age, online classes, and insightful blog posts that help you maximize your potential as a writer.

Writer's Digest (WritersDigest.com)
Another one-stop resource for everything a writer needs, including free writing advice, prompts, educational blog posts, community forums, and publishing tips that really work.

The Writing Cooperative (WritingCooperative.com)

A global community of writers who have a passion for helping and encouraging writers from around the world to work hard and develop their craft.

Medium (Medium.com)

Mentioned earlier in this book, Medium is a platform for writers of all experience levels to connect with other writers, get in front of a larger audience, get critiques, create content, get published, overcome motivation issues, build a fanbase, and more.

Reedsy (Reedsy.com)

Reedsy is an online community that helps aspiring book writers get connected to top publishing talent (designers, editors, marketers, ghostwriters, web designers, and publicists). They even offer tools such as character name generators, book formatting, and more.

Kindle Direct Publishing (kdp.Amazon.com/en_US)

One of the more popular self-publishing sites today, offering both e-books and print-on-demand options nationally and internationally.

BookBaby (BookBaby.com)

A self-publishing platform for authors with different customizable packages to help you take your book from concept to completion in no time.

Goodreads (Goodreads.com)

Goodreads touts itself as the world's largest site for readers and book recommendations. See what your friends are reading, track books you have read or want to read, and more.

AgentQuery (AgentQuery.com)

Need a literary agent to help you promote your book to the nation's top publishers? This site offers a free online database to help match you with an agent who best suits your project (fiction, nonfiction, etc.).

QueryTracker (QueryTracker.net)

Another popular online resource for book authors who need help finding an agent. New listings are being added all the time.

For Further Reading

On Writing: A Memoir of the Craft by Stephen King

Written by perhaps one of the most gifted storytellers of our time, this book is an empowering deep dive into the experiences and habits that helped shape Stephen King into the writer we all know and admire. The book lays out the basic tools of the trade every writer must have while packaging those lessons into a story everyone can relate to.

On Writing Well: The Classic Guide to Writing Nonfiction by William Zinsser

This is a classic guide to writing that helps us improve our writing and avoid many of the common mistakes that befall even the most accomplished writers.

The Elements of Style by William Strunk Jr. and E. B. White

Great for any writer, particularly when it comes to understanding and developing a keen eye for principles of composition, form, and elementary rules of usage.

**The Poets & Writers Complete Guide to Being a Better Writer
by Kevin Larimer and Mary Gannon**

This book has been labeled as the definitive source of information, insight, inspiration, and advice for creative writers. It tackles everything from how to harness your imagination to finding the right literary agent, how to market yourself, and how to find supportive writing communities.

Endnotes

Introduction

1. Steve Gamel, "Top 5 Tips for Aspiring Journalists," *Edit This* (blog), September 3, 2016, https://www.editthisllc.com/post/2016/09/03/top-5-tips-for-aspiring-journalists.

2. Gamel, "Top 5 Tips."

Chapter 1: Don't Be Afraid to Write!

1. Steve Gamel, "Why It's OK If Readers Point Out Mistakes in Your Writing," *Edit This* (blog), June 22, 2017, https://www.editthisllc.com/post /2017/06/22/why-its-ok-if-readers-point-out-mistakes-in-your-writing.

2. Gamel, "Readers Point Out Mistakes."

Chapter 2: The Aspiring Writer's Checklist

1. Steve Gamel, "Here's How Writers Can Organize the Writing Process," *Edit This* (blog), June 21, 2018, https://www.editthisllc.com/post/2018/06/16/ heres-how-writers-can-organize-the-writing-process.

2. Steve Gamel, "10 Essentials Every Writer Needs," *Edit This* (blog),

December 19, 2019, https://www.editthisllc.com/post/2019/12/19/10
-essentials-every-writer-needs.

3. Steve Gamel, "6 Tips on How to Keep Writing While You're Sick," *Edit This* (blog), May 2, 2019, https://www.editthisllc.com/post/ 2019/05/02/6-tips-on-how-to-keep-writing-while-youre-sick.

Chapter 3: Active Voice and Mechanics: Simple Ways to Improve Your Writing

1. Steve Gamel, "Improve Your Writing: Avoid Wordiness," *Edit This* (blog), November 16, 2017, https://www.editthisllc.com/post/2017/11/16/improve -your-writing-avoid-wordiness.

2. Steve Gamel, "10 Tips to Improve Your Writing," *Edit This* (blog), August 10, 2017, https://www.editthisllc.com/post/2017/08/10/10-tips -to-improve-your-writing.

Chapter 4: Why a Pen and Paper Are Still Good Tools

1. Steve Gamel, "Why Using Pen & Paper First Can Be Good for Writers," *Edit This* (blog), January 11, 2018, https://www.editthisllc.com/ post/2018/01/10/why-using-pen-paper-first-can-be-good-for-writers.

2. Gamel, "Pen & Paper First."

Chapter 5: The Hidden Messages of Writer's Block

1. Steve Gamel, "10 Hacks to Outthink Writer's Block," *Edit This* (blog), January 17, 2019, https://www.editthisllc.com/post/2019/01/17/10-hacks -to-outthink-writers-block.

2. Steve Gamel, "How My Son and His Juicy Juice Helped Me Beat Writer's Block," *Edit This* (blog), February 2, 2017, https://www.editthisllc.com/ post/2017/02/02/how-my-son-and-his-juicy-juice-helped-me-beat- writers-block.

3. Gamel, "Beat Writer's Block."

4. Steve Gamel, "Are We Better Writers by Day or Night?," *Edit This* (blog), October 12, 2016, https://www.editthisllc.com/post/2016/10/12/are-we-better-writers-by-day-or-night.

5. Gamel, "Better Writers by Day?"

6. Steve Gamel, "4 Reasons Why Writer's Block Can Be a Good Thing," *Edit This* (blog), February 9, 2017, https://www.editthisllc.com/post/2017/02/09/4-reasons-why-writers-block-can-be-a-good-thing.

7. Steve Gamel, "10 Time Management Tips for Writers," *Edit This* (blog), January 18, 2018, https://www.editthisllc.com/post/2018/01/18/10-time-management-tips-for-writers.

8. Gamel, "4 Reasons Writer's Block."

9. Gamel, "4 Reasons Writer's Block."

10. Steve Gamel, "25 Easy Ways to Stay Inspired as a Writer," *Edit This* (blog), April 27, 2017, https://www.editthisllc.com/post/2017/04/27/25-easy-ways-to-stay-inspired-as-a-writer.

Chapter 7: How Active Listening Can Make You a Better Journalist

1. Steve Gamel, "10 Interview Tips and Techniques for Writers," *Edit This* (blog), August 3, 2017, https://www.editthisllc.com/post/2017/08/03/10-interview-tips-and-techniques-for-writers.

2. Gamel, "10 Interview Tips."

3. Steve Gamel, "Top 5 Tips for Aspiring Journalists," *Edit This* (blog), September 3, 2016, https://www.editthisllc.com/post/2016/09/03/top-5-tips-for-aspiring-journalists.

Chapter 8: Research and Organization: The Hallmarks of Good Nonfiction

1. Tim Stevenson, *Better: The Fundamentals of Leadership* (San Bernadino, California: Stevenson Leadership Coaching, 2016), 198.

2. Rebecca Skloot, *The Immortal Life of Henrietta Lacks* (New York: Crown Publishing Group, 2010), 1.

Chapter 10: Storytelling: Not Just for Novelists

1. Steve Gamel, "Concussions: Breaking the Cycle," *Denton Record-Chronicle* (Denton, TX), February 19, 2017.

2. Steve Gamel, "Argyle Star Gray to Sign with Fort Lewis," *Denton Record-Chronicle* (Denton, TX), November 9, 2016.

3. Steve Gamel, "Tips on Writing a Great Lede (or Lead): Are You Doing It Right?," *Edit This* (blog), November 17, 2016, https://www.editthisllc.com/post/2016/11/17/tips-on-writing-a-great-lede-or-lead-are-you-doing-it-right.

4. Steve Gamel, "4 Reasons Why Being an Extrovert Can Make You a Better Writer," *Edit This* (blog), January 19, 2017, https://www.editthisllc.com/post/2017/01/19/4-reasons-why-being-an-extrovert-can-make-you-a-better-writer.

Chapter 11: Becoming a Successful Freelance Writer

1. Steve Gamel, "6 Ways Freelance Writers Can Get Noticed by Potential Clients," *Edit This* (blog), February 27, 2020, https://www.editthisllc.com/post/2020/02/27/6-ways-freelance-writers-can-get-noticed-by-potential-clients.

2. Gamel, "6 Ways Freelance Writers."

3. STRIKE Baseball, "STRIKE Coaches," *STRIKE Performance*, 2017, strikebaseballtraining.com/coaching-staff/.

4. Gamel, "6 Ways Freelance Writers."

5. Steve Gamel, "6 Social Media Tips from a Small-Business Owner," *Edit This* (blog), February 28, 2019, https://www.editthisllc.com/post/2019/02/28/6-social-media-tips-from-a-small-business-owner.

6. Gamel, "6 Ways Freelance Writers."

Chapter 12: Honoring the Editing Process

1. Steve Gamel, "Editing, Copy Editing, Proofreading: Do You Know the Difference?," *Edit This* (blog), January 5, 2017, https://www.editthisllc.com/post/2017/01/05/editing-copy-editing-proofreading-do-you-know-the-difference.

2. Steve Gamel, "Self-Editing Is Self-Sabotage: 4 Reasons Why Writers Need Editors," *Edit This* (blog), December 15, 2016, https://www.editthisllc.com/post/2016/12/15/self-editing-is-self-sabotage-4-reasons-writers-need-editors.

3. Steve Gamel, "6 Tips to Help You Edit Your Own Writing," *Edit This* (blog), July 18, 2019, https://www.editthisllc.com/post/2019/07/18/6-tips-to-help-you-edit-your-own-writing.

4. Gamel, "Edit Your Own Writing."

5. Steve Gamel, "Edit This Grammar Lesson: Is It Wrong to Start a Sentence with And or But?," *Edit This* (blog), April 30, 2020, https://www.editthisllc.com/post/2020/04/30/edit-this-grammar-lesson-is-it-wrong-to-start-a-sentence-with-and-or-but.

6. Steve Gamel, "4 Older Grammar Rules That I Don't Mind Breaking Every So Often," *Edit This* (blog), May 21, 2020, https://www.editthisllc.com/post/2020/05/21/4-older-grammar-rules-that-i-don-t-mind-breaking-every-so-often.

Chapter 13: Marketing Your Work

1. Steve Gamel, "How to Be Better at Networking When Networking Isn't Your Thing," *Edit This* (blog), June 29, 2017, https://www.editthisllc.com/post/2017/06/29/how-to-be-better-at-networking-when-networking-isnt-your-thing.

About the Author

Steve Gamel is an award-winning writer, journalist, and communicator. That's the buttoned-up, professional part. At his heart, however, he is just a fun-loving, humble kid from Texas whose passion for the written word and quality, down-to-earth storytelling knows no limits.

Originally imagining himself a future sportscaster, Steve realized during his time as a broadcast journalism student at the University of North Texas that his true calling wasn't television but rather the pages of newspapers and magazines. He has immersed himself in the intricacies of the craft over the past two-plus decades, all the while being humble enough to take on any assignment, learn all he can from the accomplished writers and editors who came before him, and recognize that becoming the best writer he can be is a lifelong endeavor. With this book, Steve's goal is to connect with other writers, share what he's learned, and have a real conversation about writing, writers, and how we can master our passion for the written word.

In his free time, Steve enjoys spending time with his wife and two sons, watching sports, and being around people. He lives in Denton, Texas.